FOR MY AUN

CREATIVE PATTERNS

COLOURING FOR GROWN-UPS

MIA HARPER

BrightBoldPublishing

Published by Bright Bold Publishing in 2015
First Edition, First Printing

Illustrations and cover design © 2015 Mia Harper
http://brightboldpublishing.com

ALL RIGHTS RESERVED

No part of this book may be reproduced or transmitted in any form or by any means, including but not limited to information storage and retrieval systems, electronic, mechanical, photocopy, recording, etc, without written permission from Bright Bold Publishing.

ISBN (Paperback)
978-1-911045-13-7

TO CONTACT BRIGHT BOLD PUBLISHING

Visit BrightBoldPublishing.com or send an email to Mia@BrightBoldPublishing.com

DEDICATION

All my thanks go to my family who
have shown amazing restraint and patience
while I have had a great time creating
my colouring books

DESIGN STYLES

COLOUR TO CALM – BE CREATIVE

Do you find you need to switch off from the noisy world and find your own quiet corner of calm?

If this is you there's no better way than to pick up this amazing adult colouring book of 30 designs to help you escape from the day's pressures. You'll become engrossed in these patterns for meditative colouring.

The colouring book for grownups has abstract, traditional and geometric patterns.

As you colour it'll keep you focussed in the present moment and allow your creative side to emerge.

When you become absorbed in the colouring of shapes and patterns you'll unleash your creative juices and imaginative powers. You'll feel a sense of satisfaction and fulfilment at having completed a unique piece of art. Even better, over time, you'll have compiled a fantastic collection of art to be proud of, frame and decorate your walls with.

You can share this pastime with your family and friends or connect with your colouring book groups. Or, if you just want to spend some 'me-time' alone, that's okay! No drawing experience is required to create your own exceptional designs. You're free to sink into the rhythm of the shapes and lines.

For the marker enthusiasts, who love bright, vivid colours that boost your mood and uplift the soul, these designs have been created with you in mind.

You can achieve stunning results with the minimum of colours. Or if you want to walk on the 'wild' side use as many colours as you dare.

CHECK OUT THE OTHER BOOKS IN THE COLLECTION

See Mia's colouring books for grown-ups. A great gift for the wonderful person in your life. Stunning patterns to colour.

For My Gran
For My Mum
For My Daughter
For My Sister
For My Wife
For My Auntie
For My Niece
For My Sister-in-Law
For My Girlfriend

SEE THE MANDALA COLLECTION

48 traditional, geometrical and abstract designs.

Bold & Beautiful
Bold & Gorgeous
Bold & Distinct
Bold & Divergent
Bold & Individual
Bold & Special

You can see inside each book for styles before purchasing.

Don't delay. ORDER Today

HINTS AND TIPS

Pull this book apart or photocopy the heart patterns onto a quality weight of paper that will work in your printer.

If you choose to colour in your book place a piece of card behind the design to avoid bleed through the paper.

Brilliant vivid markers are recommended as most of the patterns have dark lines. Strong bright colours will enhance the design.

Use Staedtler triplus fineliner, 0.3 mm - 20 Brilliant Colours for small shapes and Staedtler 20 triplus colours, 1.0 mm, for larger areas.

If you are into experimenting with colours buying a cheaper range of fibre tip pens from a supermarket in a 20 pack might do the trick. These are normally for children but you can get comparable colours though it might require you to press a little harder to get the ink flowing.

For those in the UK Sainsbury's great budget purchase of 18 pack brush markers are a good compromise. Colours are strong and vibrant and you need only apply a gentle pressure. If you press too hard you'll mash the paper fibres.

My favourite range is Djeco double ended pens. 10 per pack. You get rich hues from the felt brush and fibre tipped nibs. The ink flow is excellent. I discovered these at Hobbycraft in the UK.

Turquoise, yellow, orange, pink and bright green help highlight areas of your design.

When applying colours to larger areas of your work start with gentle fine strokes as if you were painting the surface. Go over the area again if you want to make the colour stronger. Using a light touch will help you avoid making mistakes.

Choosing colours and deciding what goes well together can be daunting. To get an appreciation of colours that work check this free website out http://www.sessions.edu/color-calculator. There are some great tutorials on colour combinations and the colour wheel.

Another way to check out colour combinations is to look at other people's artwork and model what they have done.

Mia Harper
Author/Designer

Mia Harper lives in North West England. She has a real passion for Art Nouveau, Art Deco, the Edwardian, Victorian, Georgian and Renaissance periods of art.

She is a qualified Graphic Designer who lived and worked in London spending many years training other professionals in some of the top companies and advertising agencies helping them create magazines, brochures and leaflets.

When she returned to the North West she decided to stop training others and spend more time developing her own designs.

Needing to instil a manageable work life balance and address some personal issues she sought help through mindfulness therapy which set her on the road to practising living in the now.

She has produced a collection of adult colouring books and writes children's fiction.

See her Colouring Books for grownups under the Bold range,

Get the ideal Christmas, birthday or Valentine's gift. Colouring books filled with great patterns for the special person in your life.

For my Gran	For my Sister	For my Niece
For my Mum	For my Wife	For my Sister-in-law
For my Daughter	For my Auntie	For my Girlfriend

You can find Mia at Brightboldpublishing.com and @MiaHarper007

THE FLOWER GARDEN PROJECT

CREATING A GARDEN OF FLOWERS

Create a large frieze with several flowers or a small picture with one or two flowers. Produce a background for the frieze or picture. It can be a coloured background but try and keep it simple as the flowers will be very detailed in their varied colours.

1. Select heart patterns and photocopy them onto a good quality paper
2. Colour them either yourself or with a group of friends
3. You can also mix and match patterns
4. Form a flower shape with the hearts
5. Use two and three hearts to create other shaped flowers
6. Add leaves and stems to the flower shapes

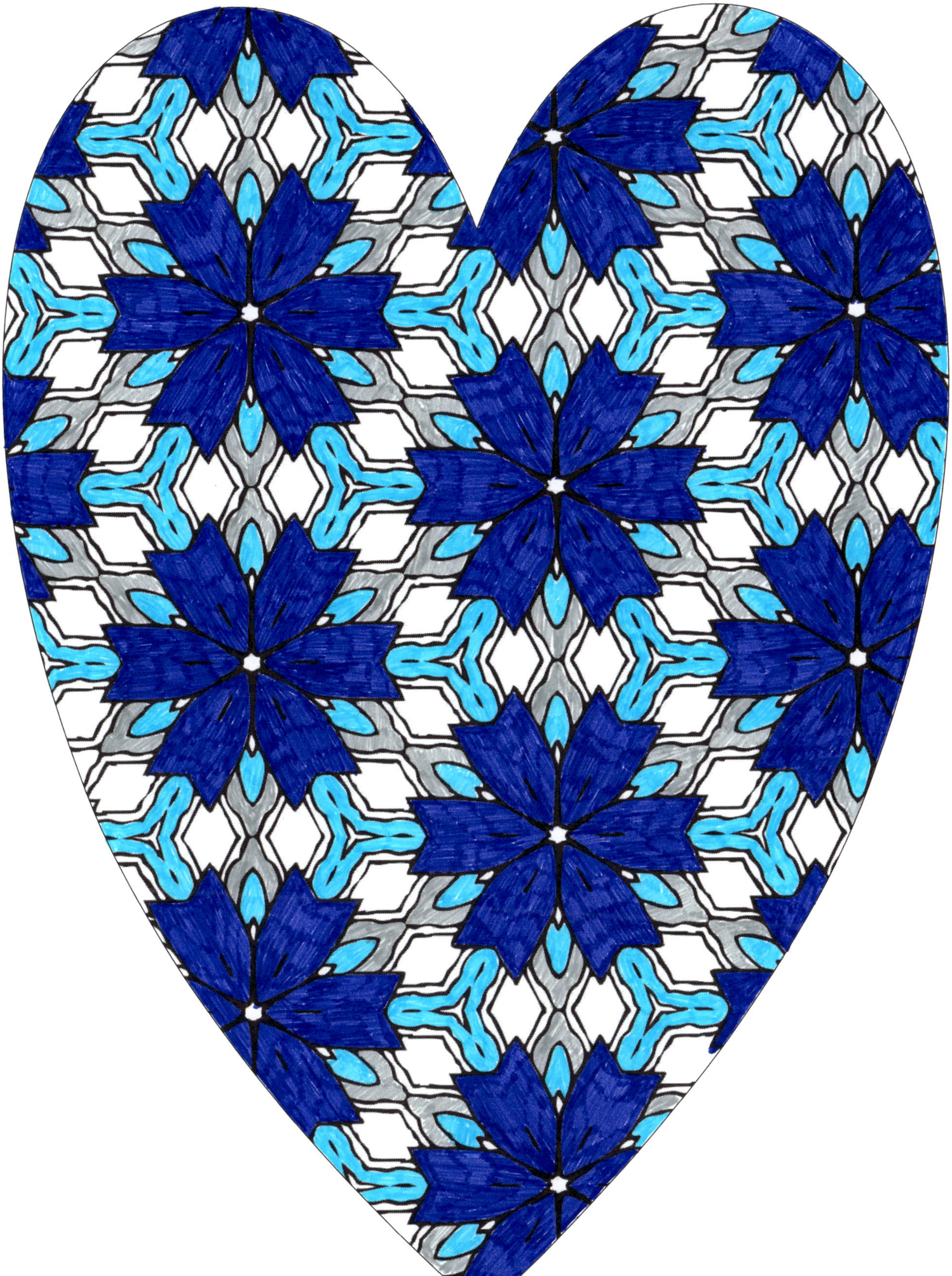

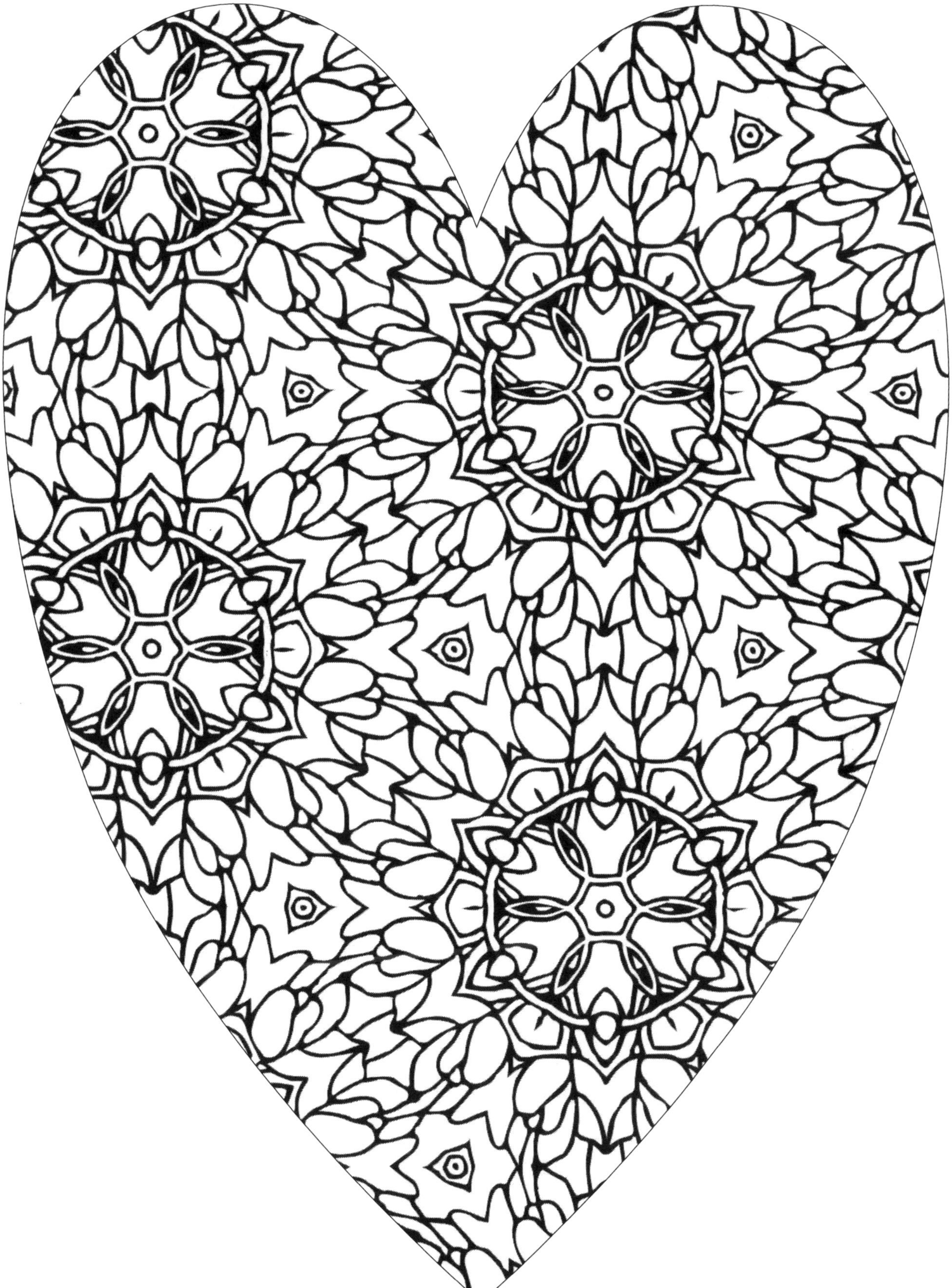

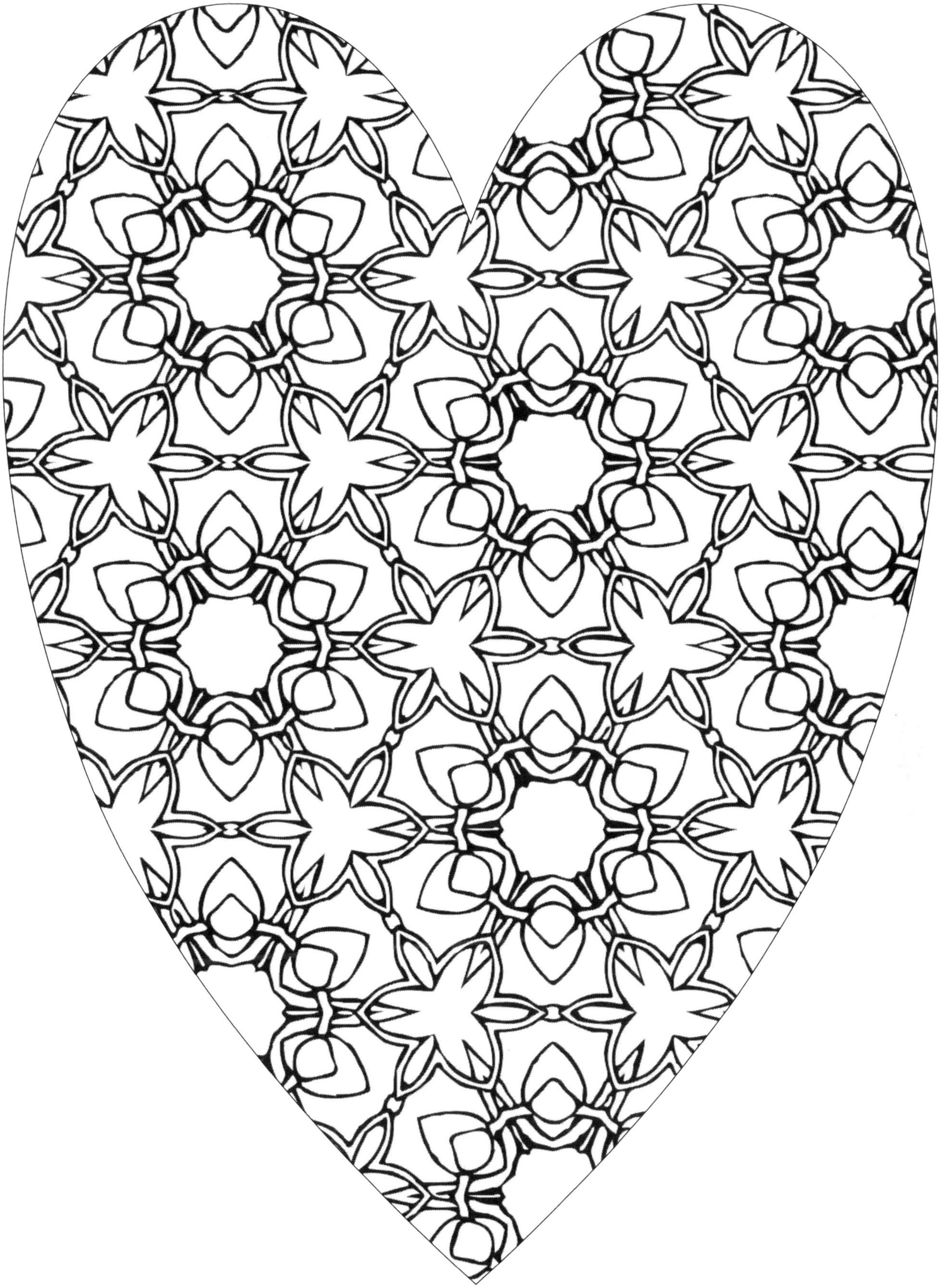

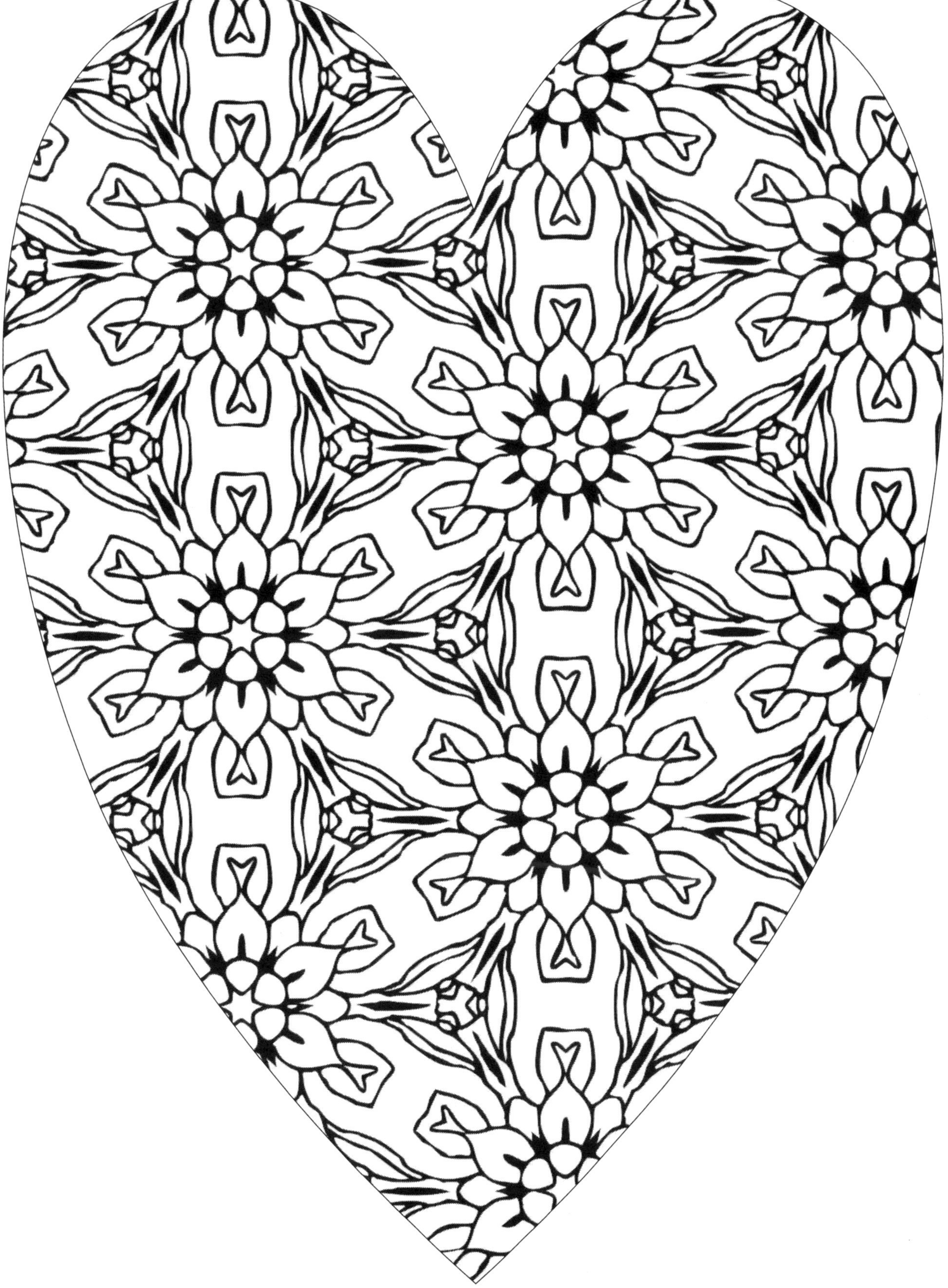

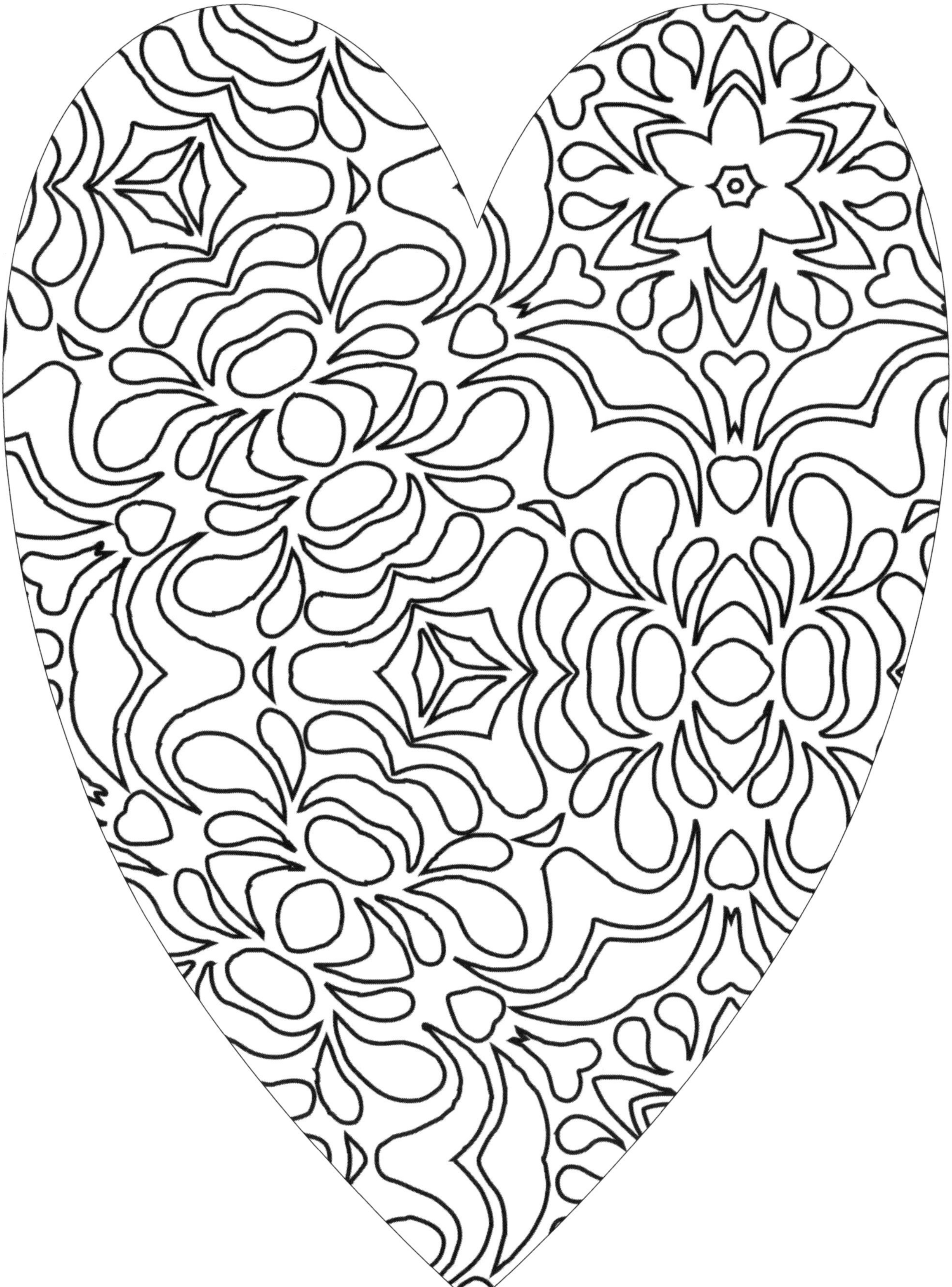

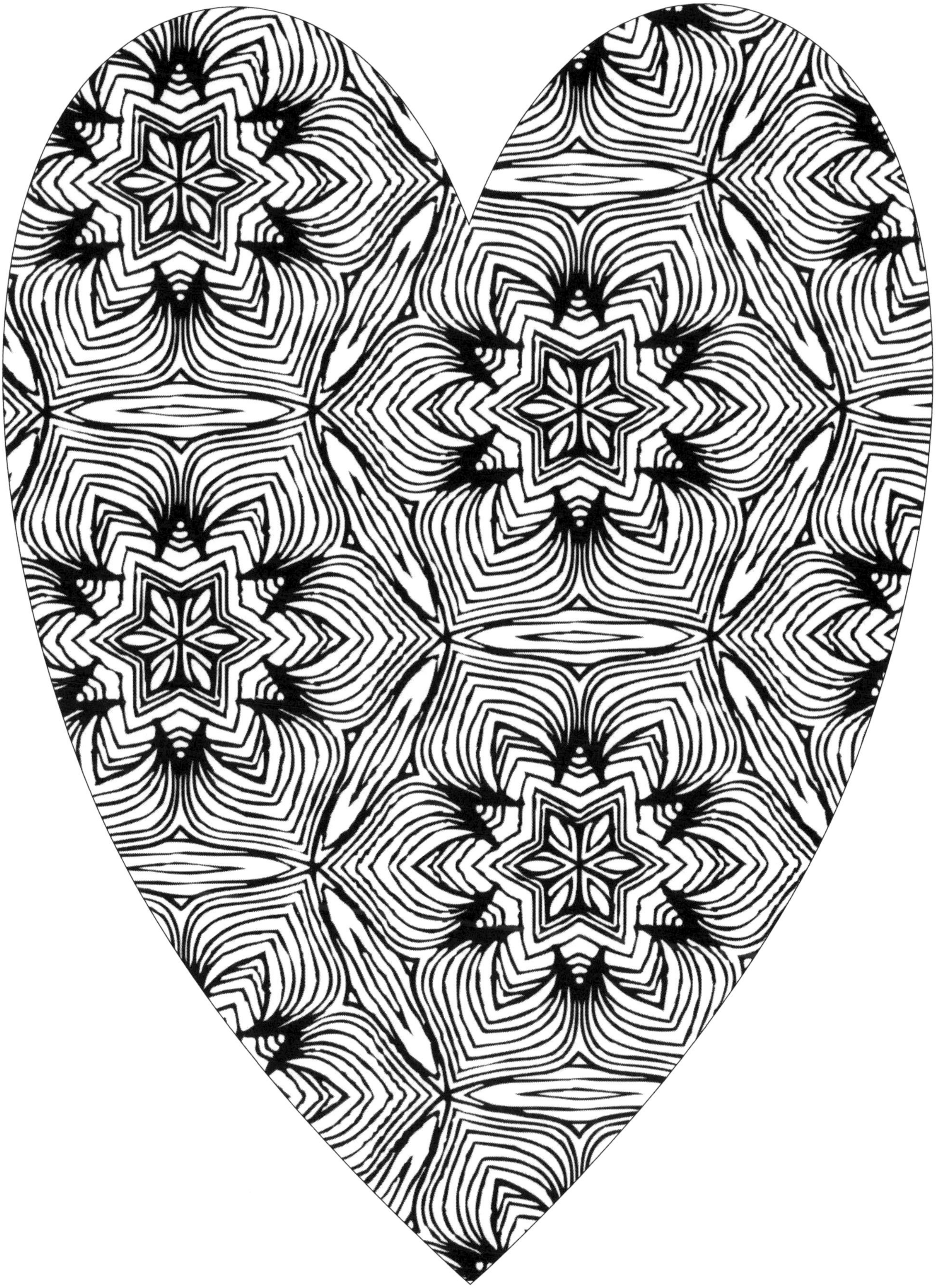

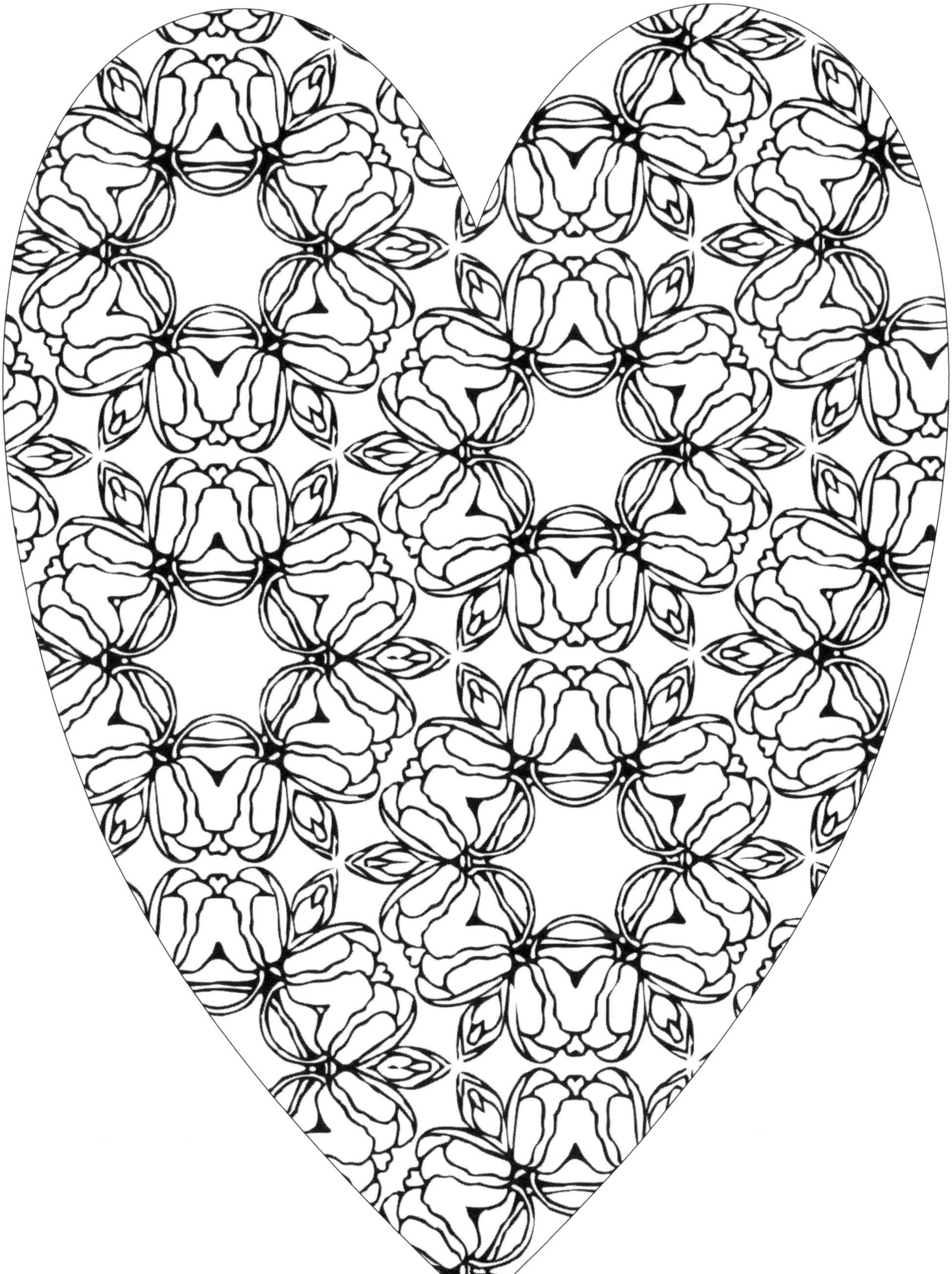

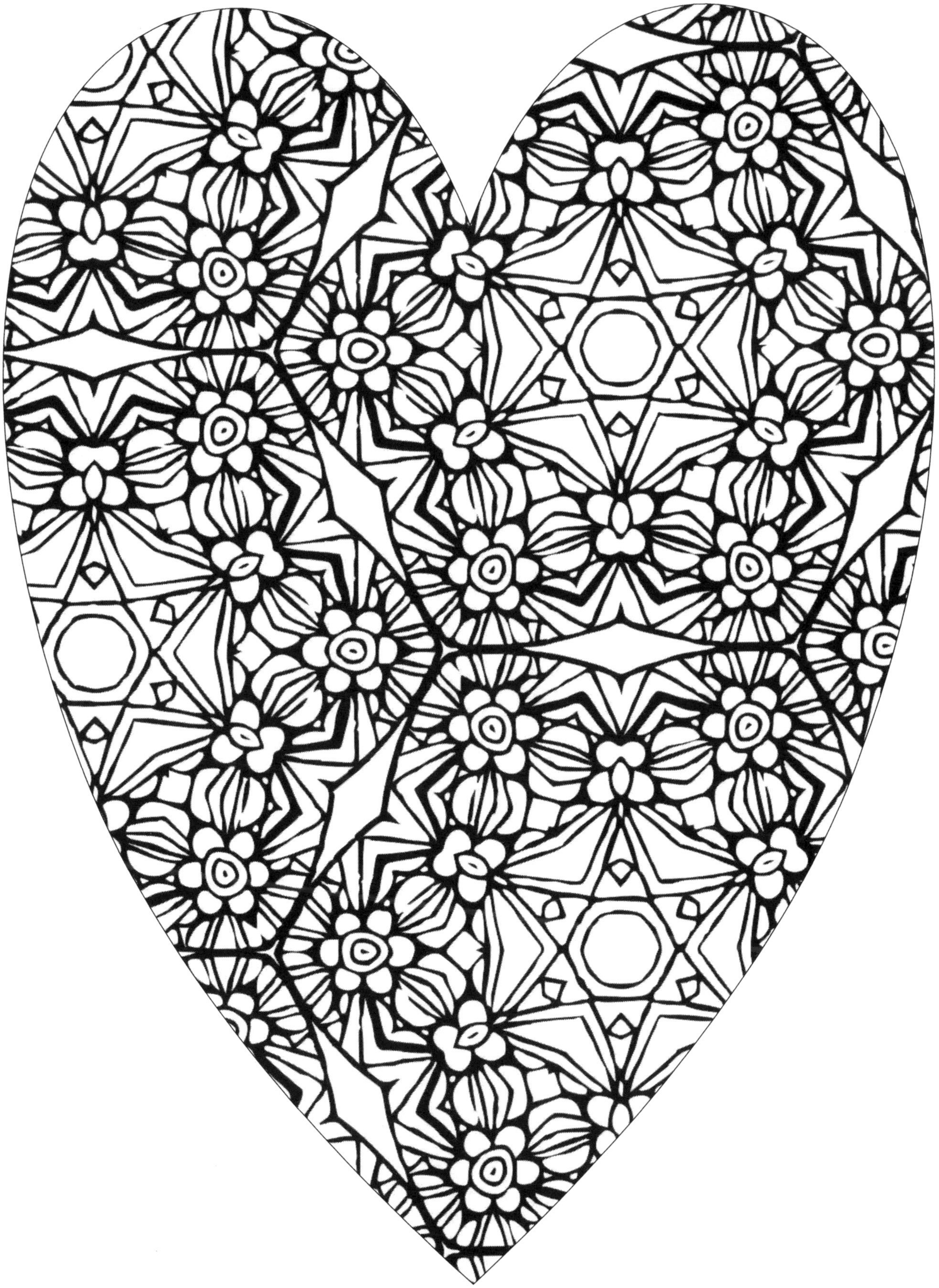

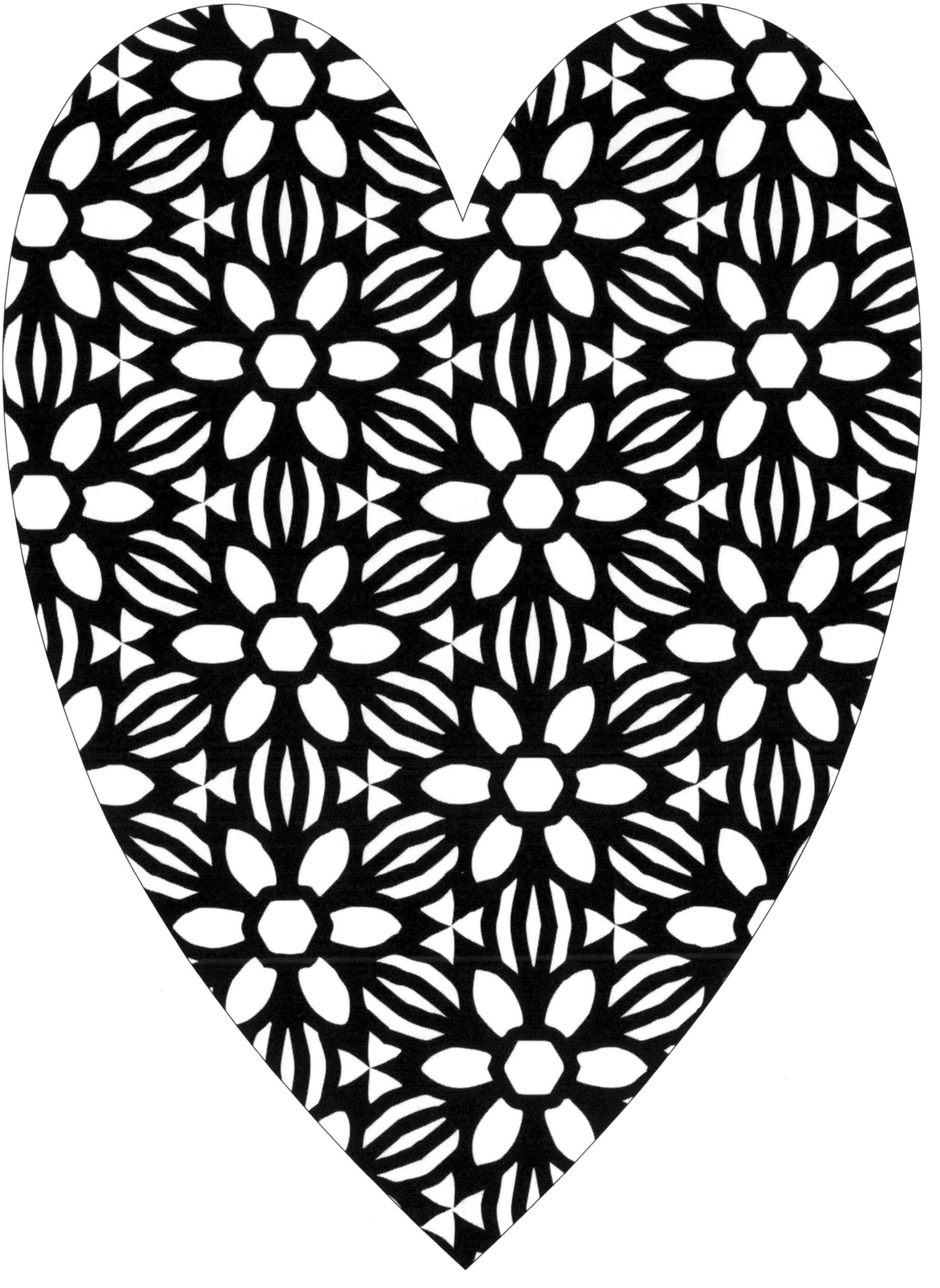

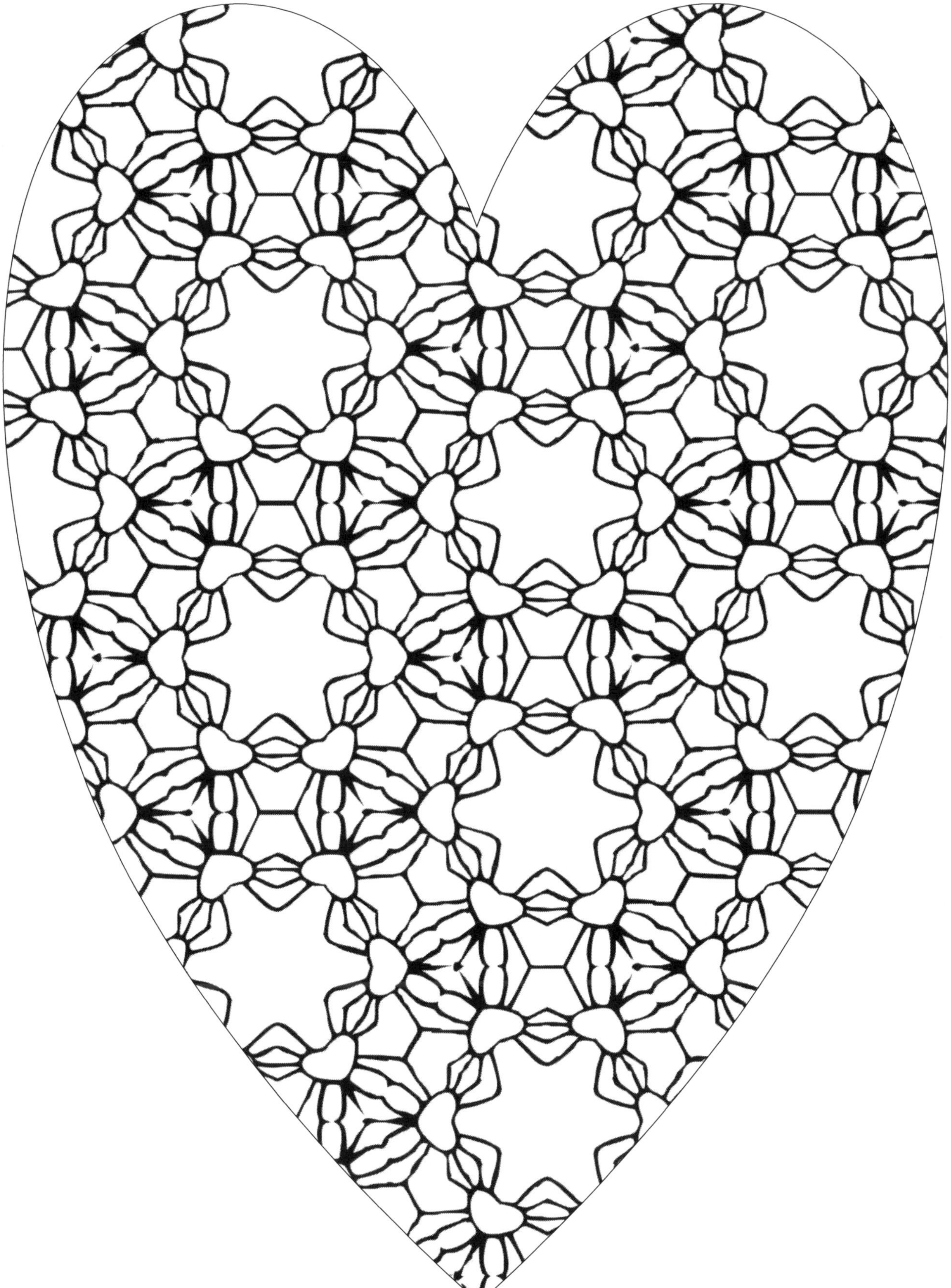

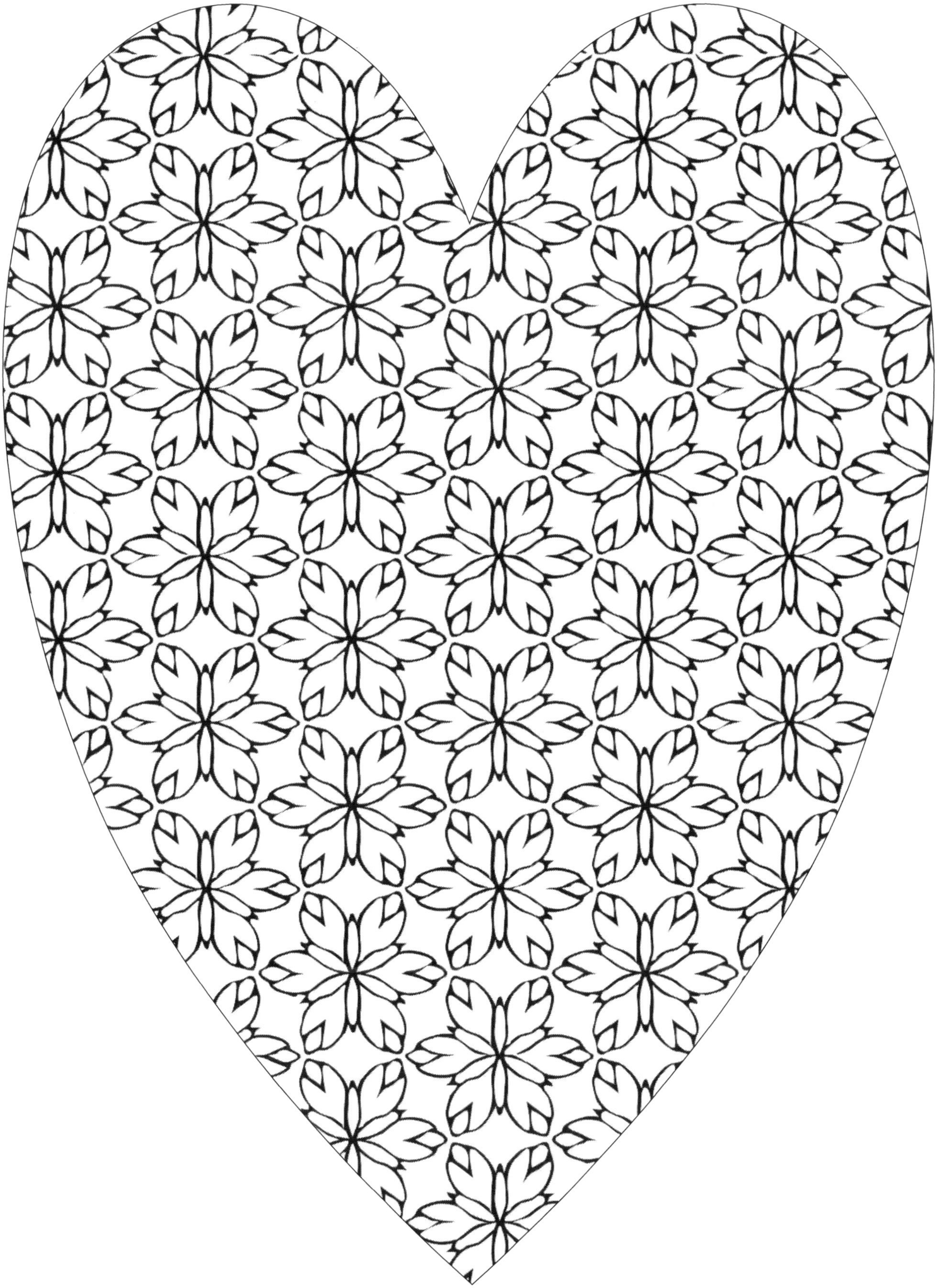

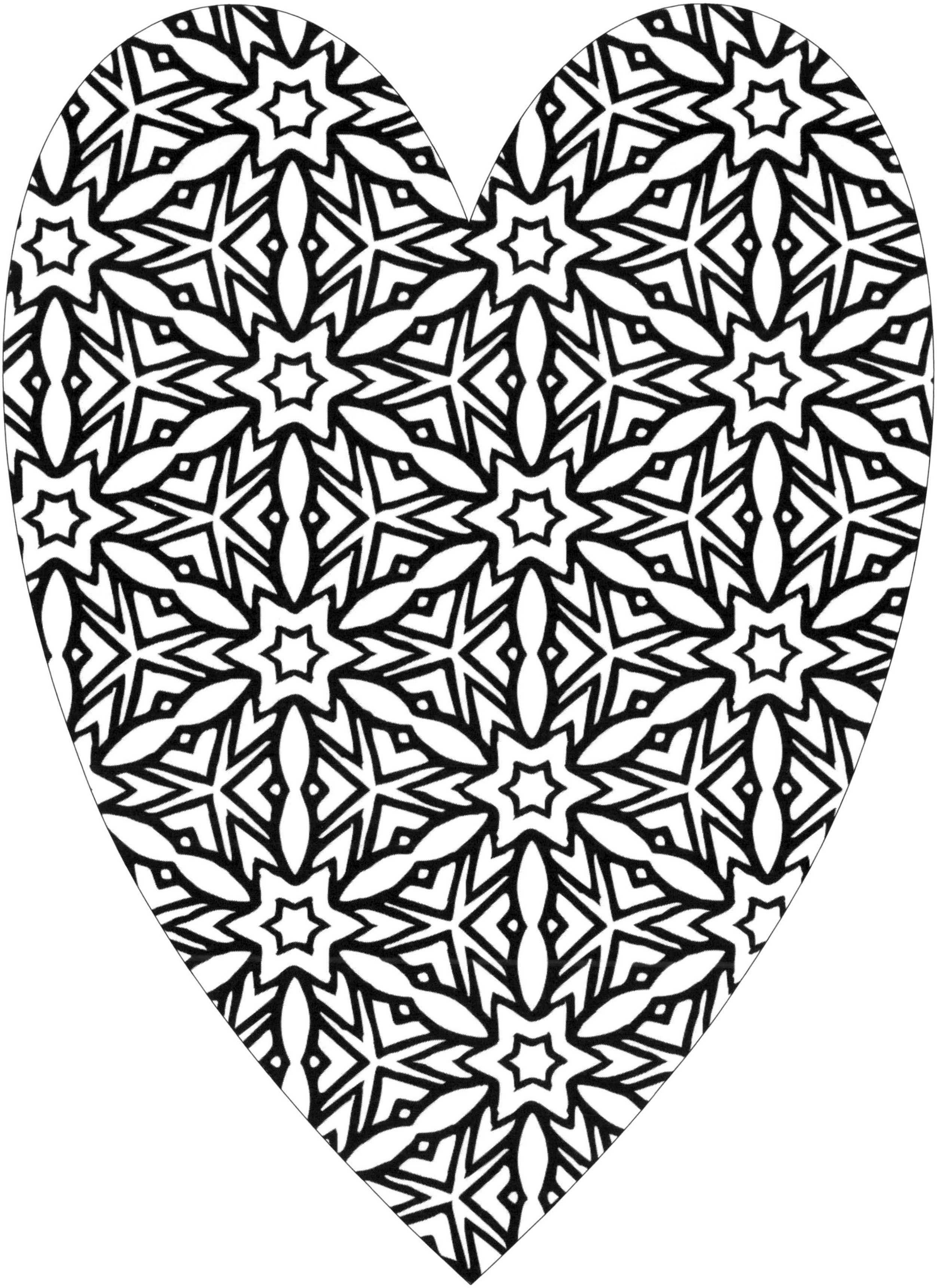

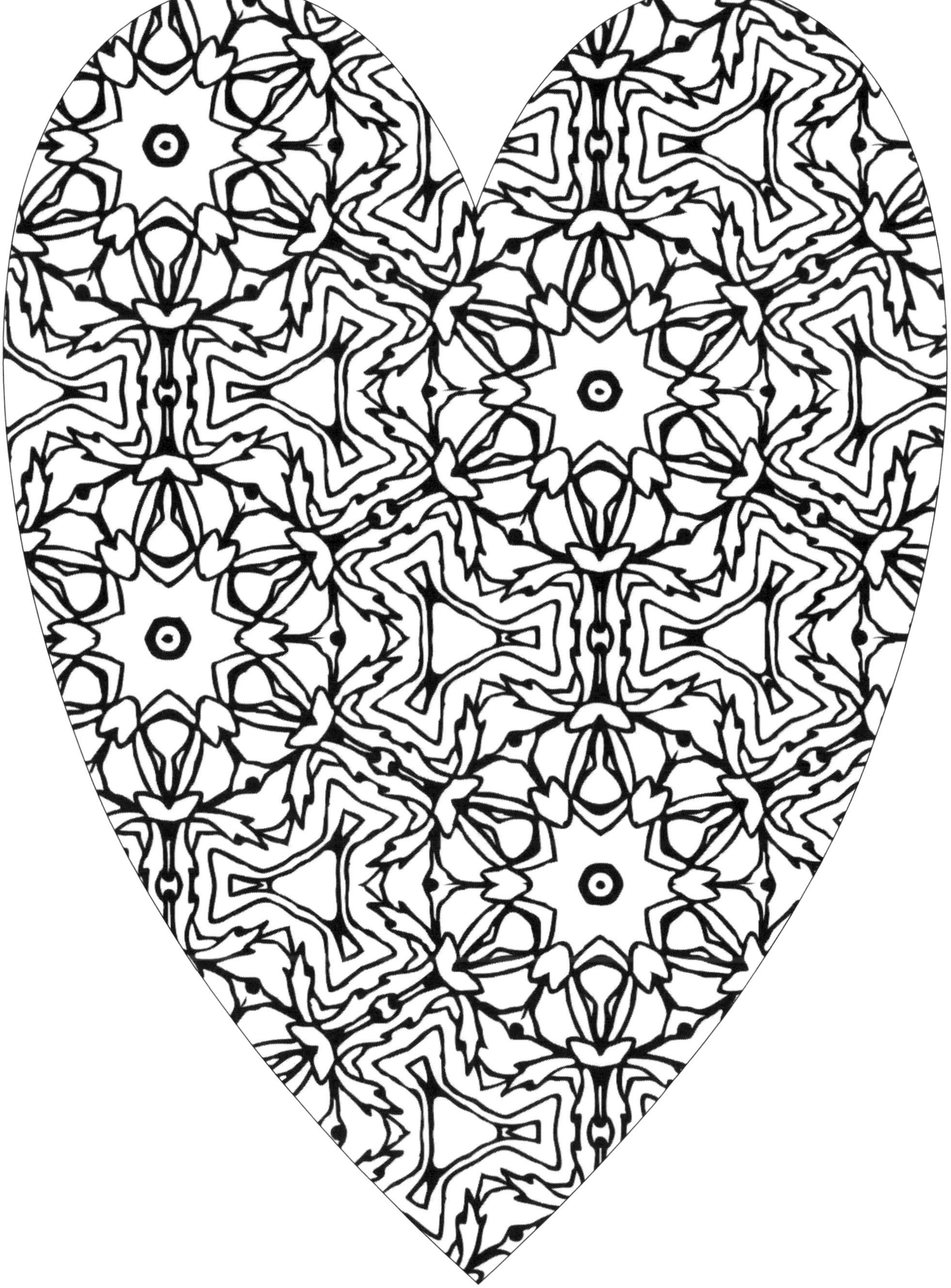

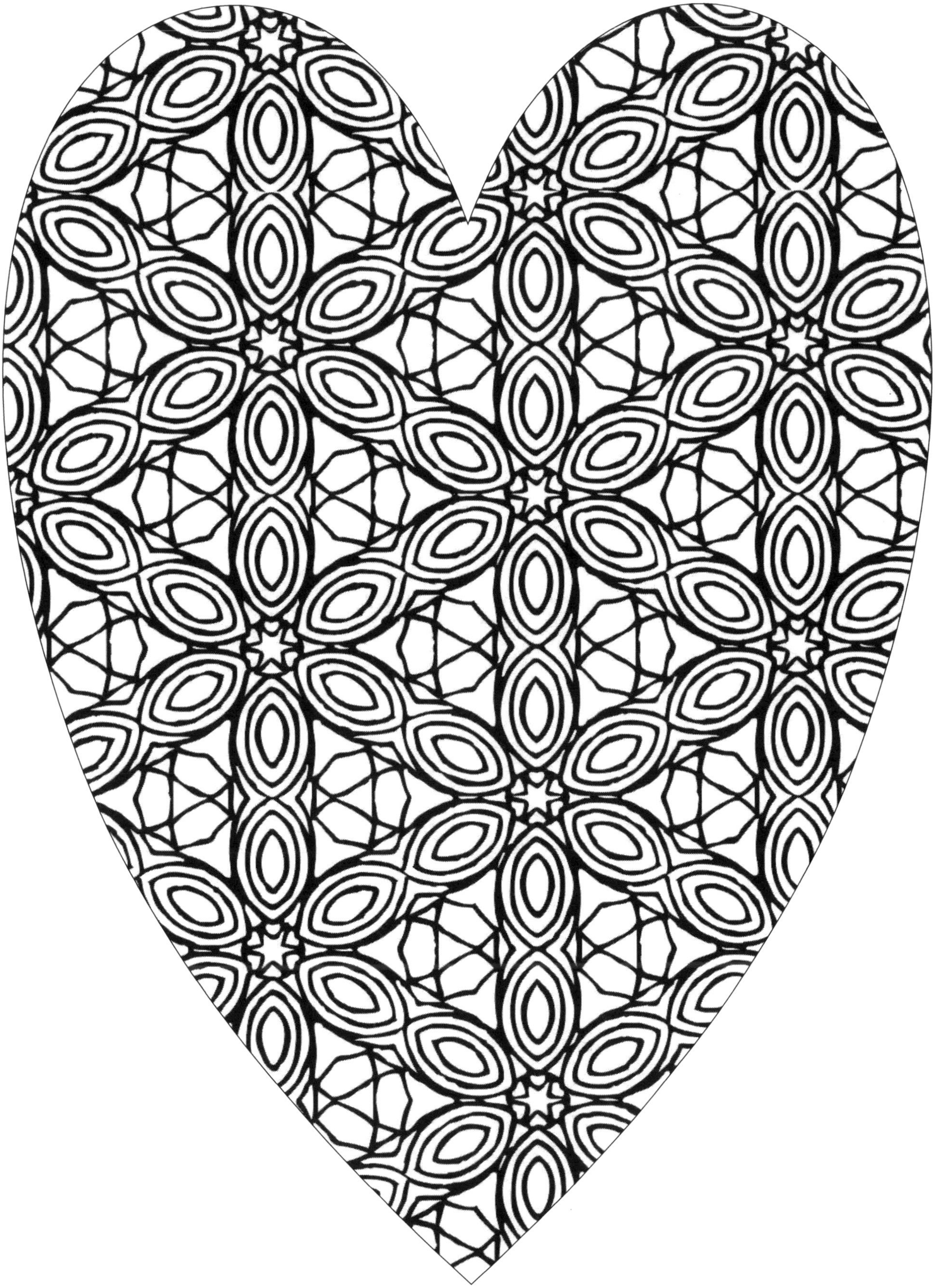

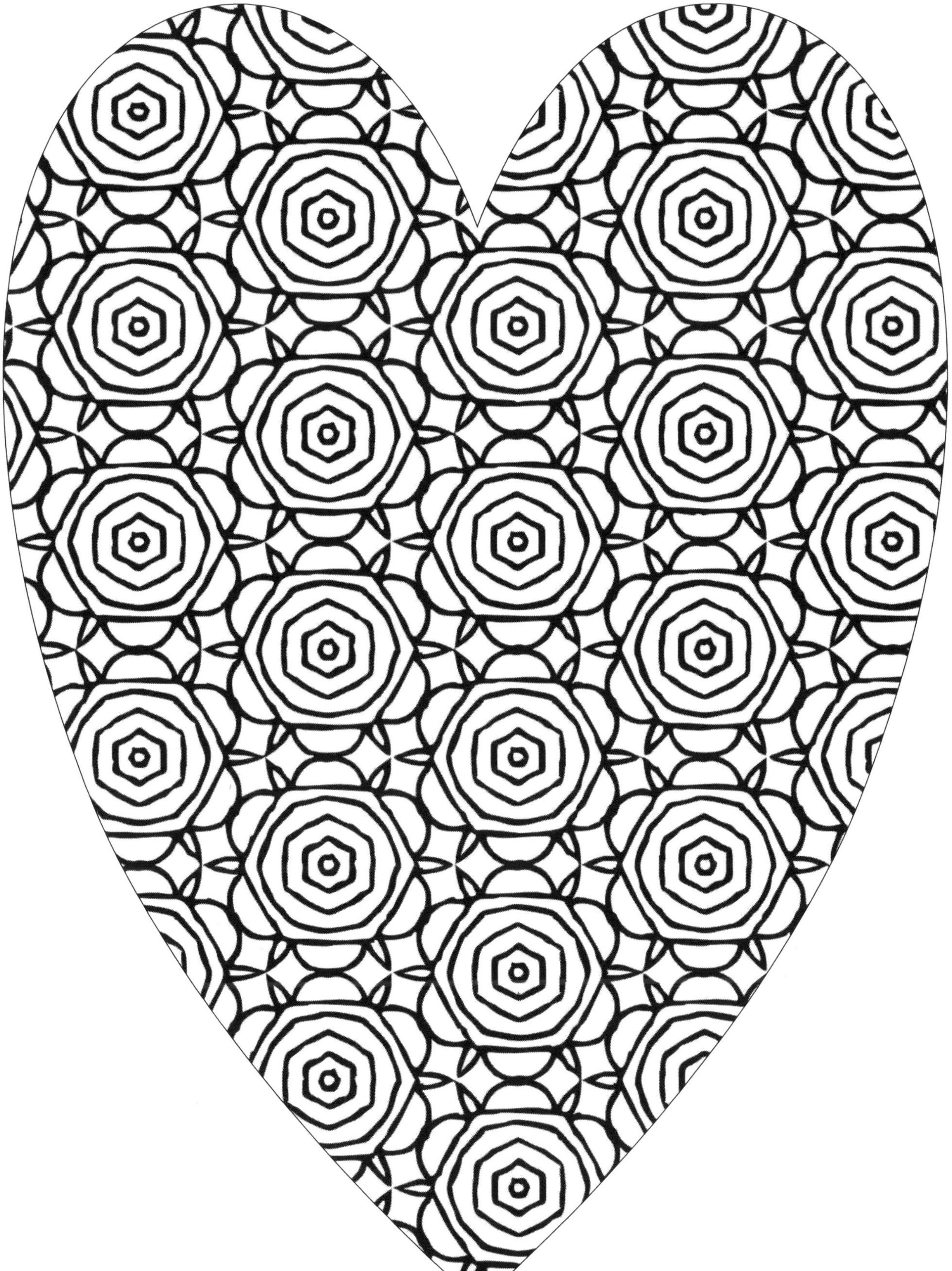

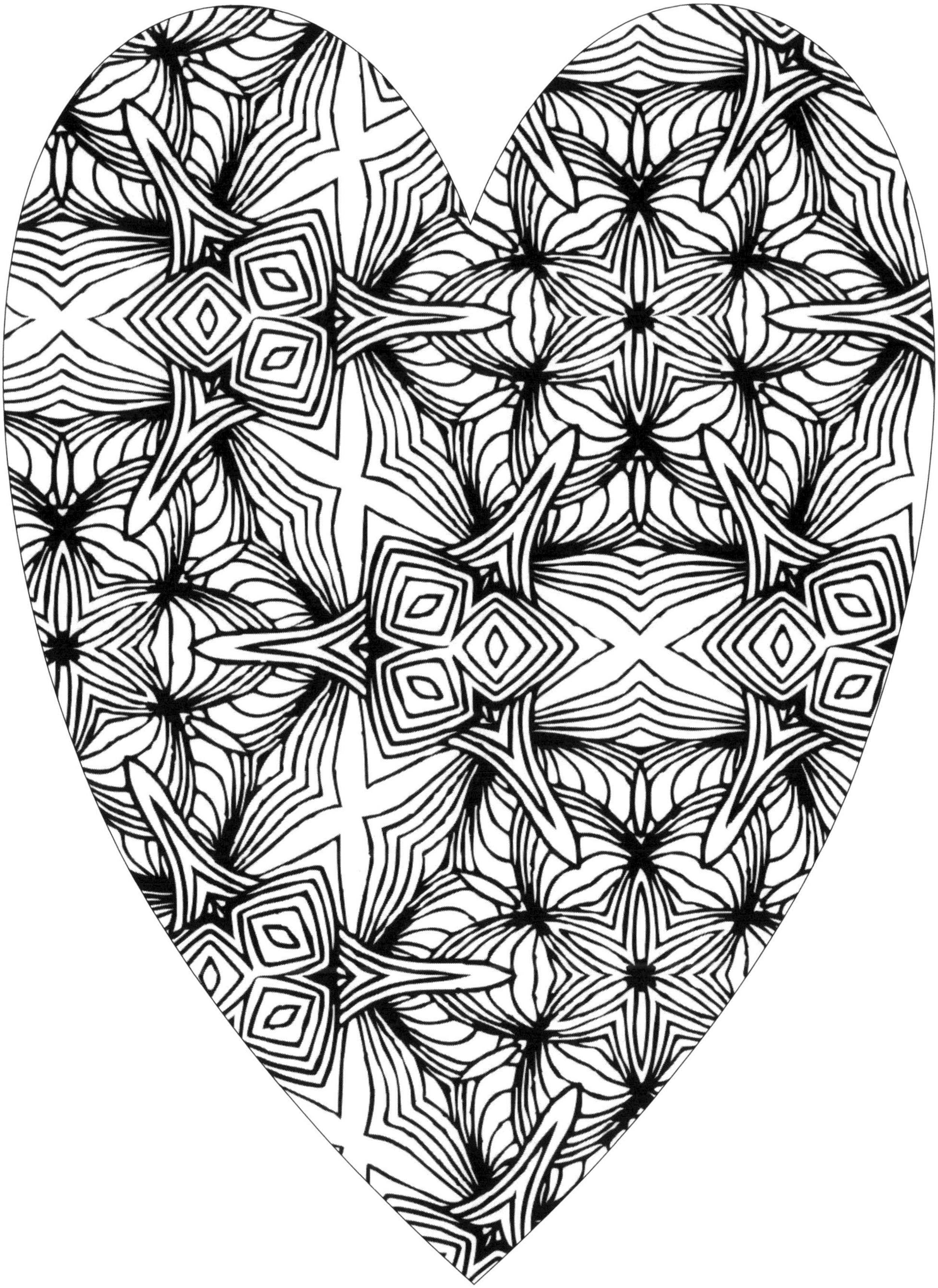

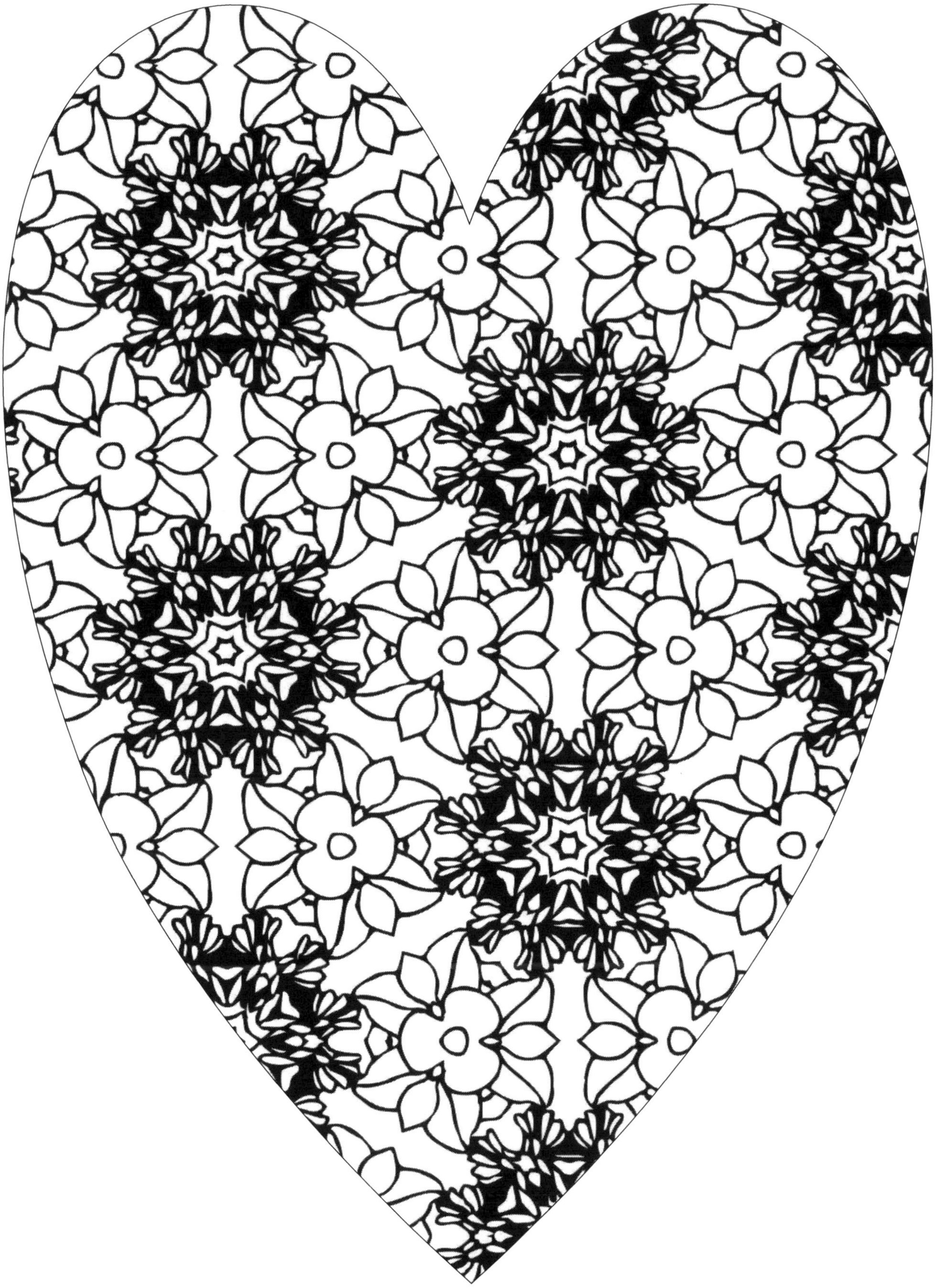

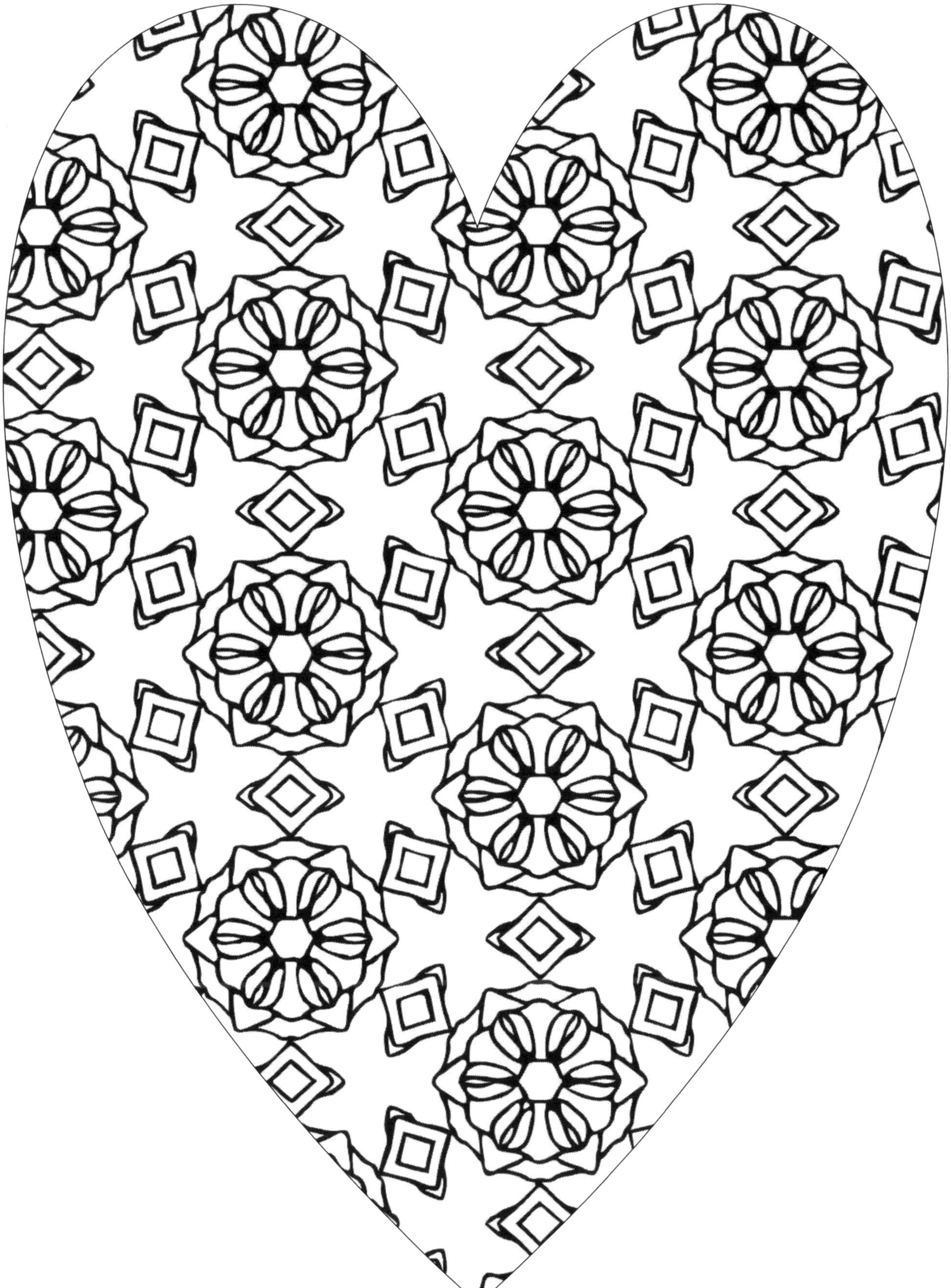

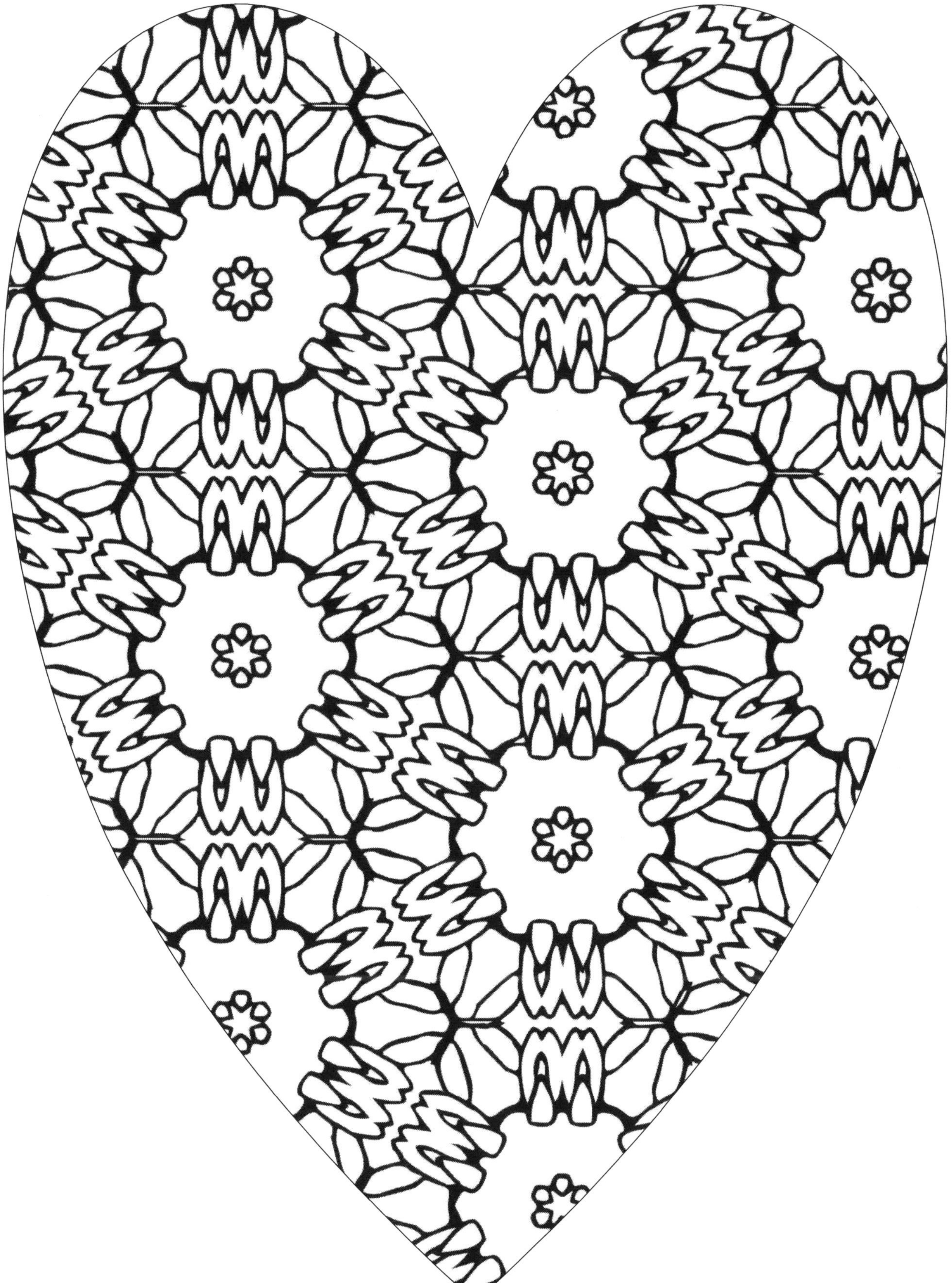

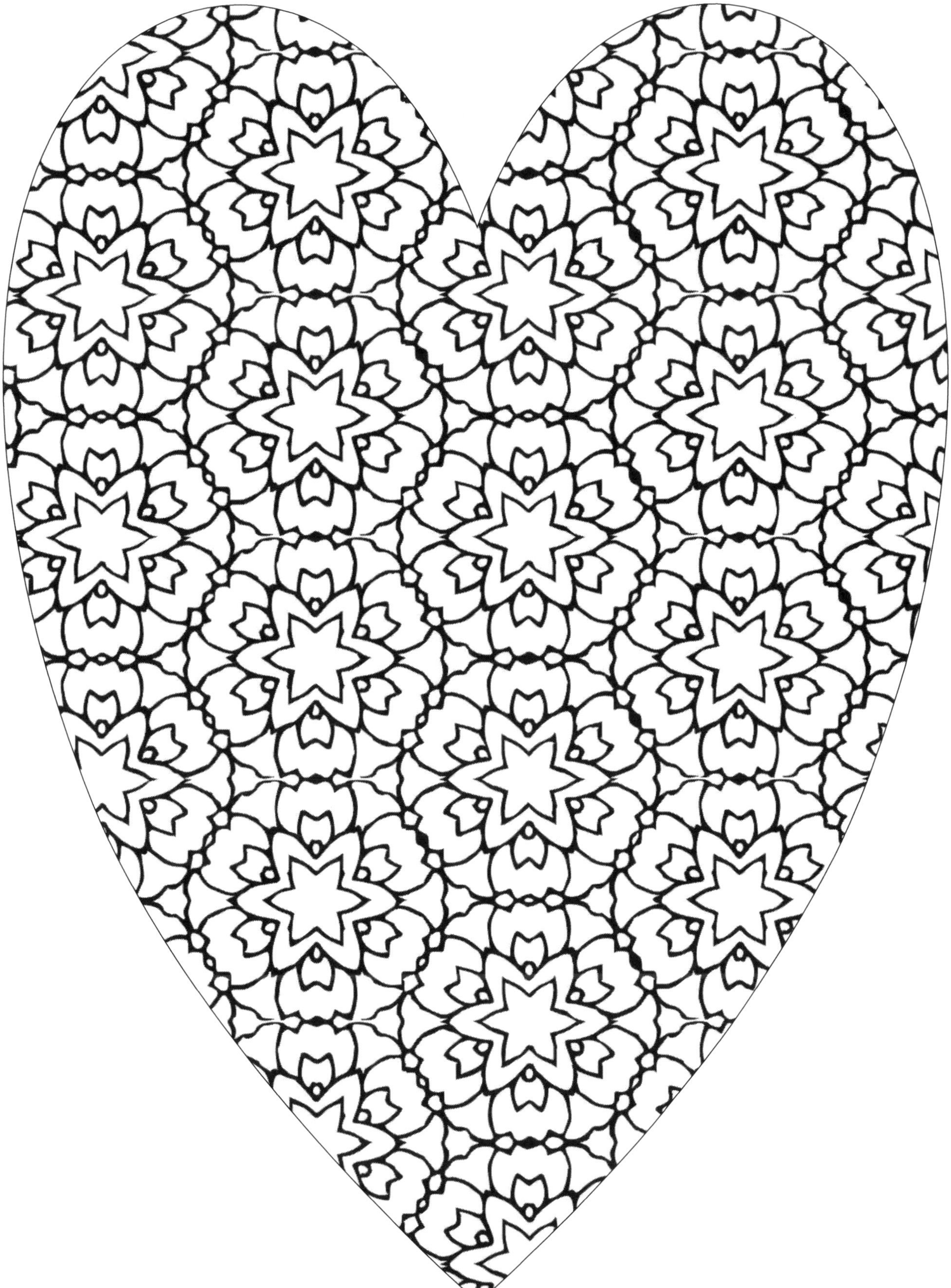

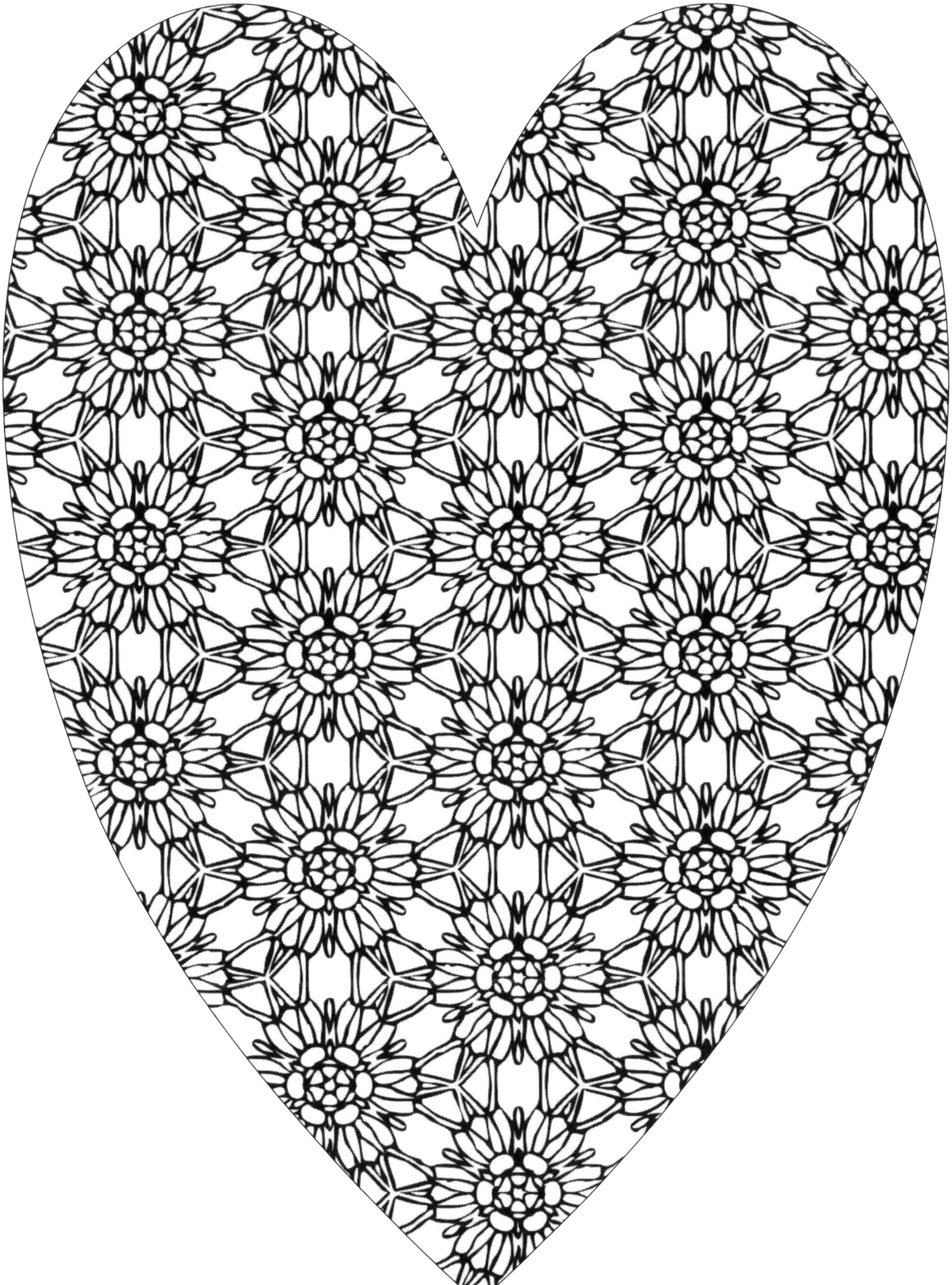

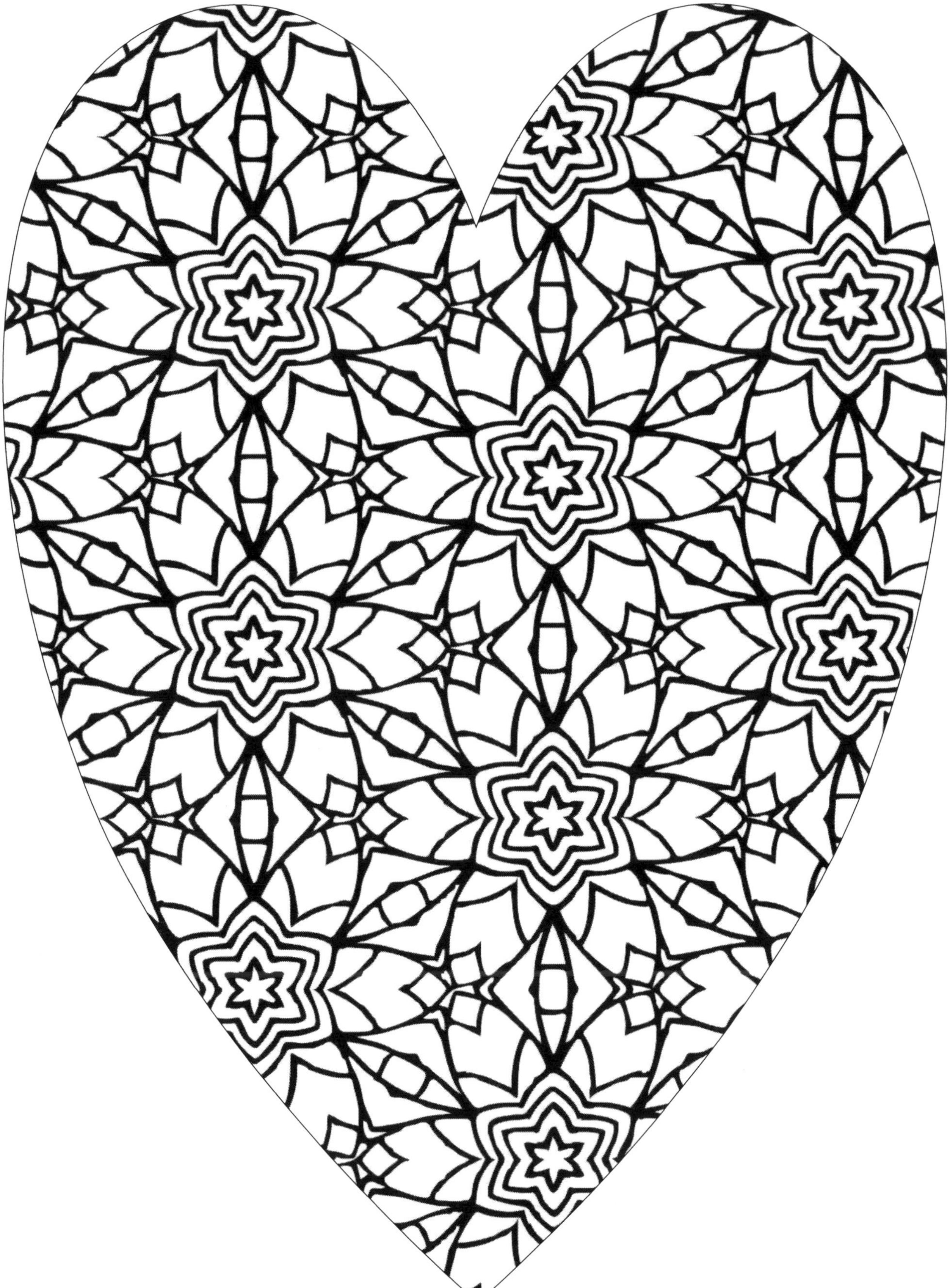

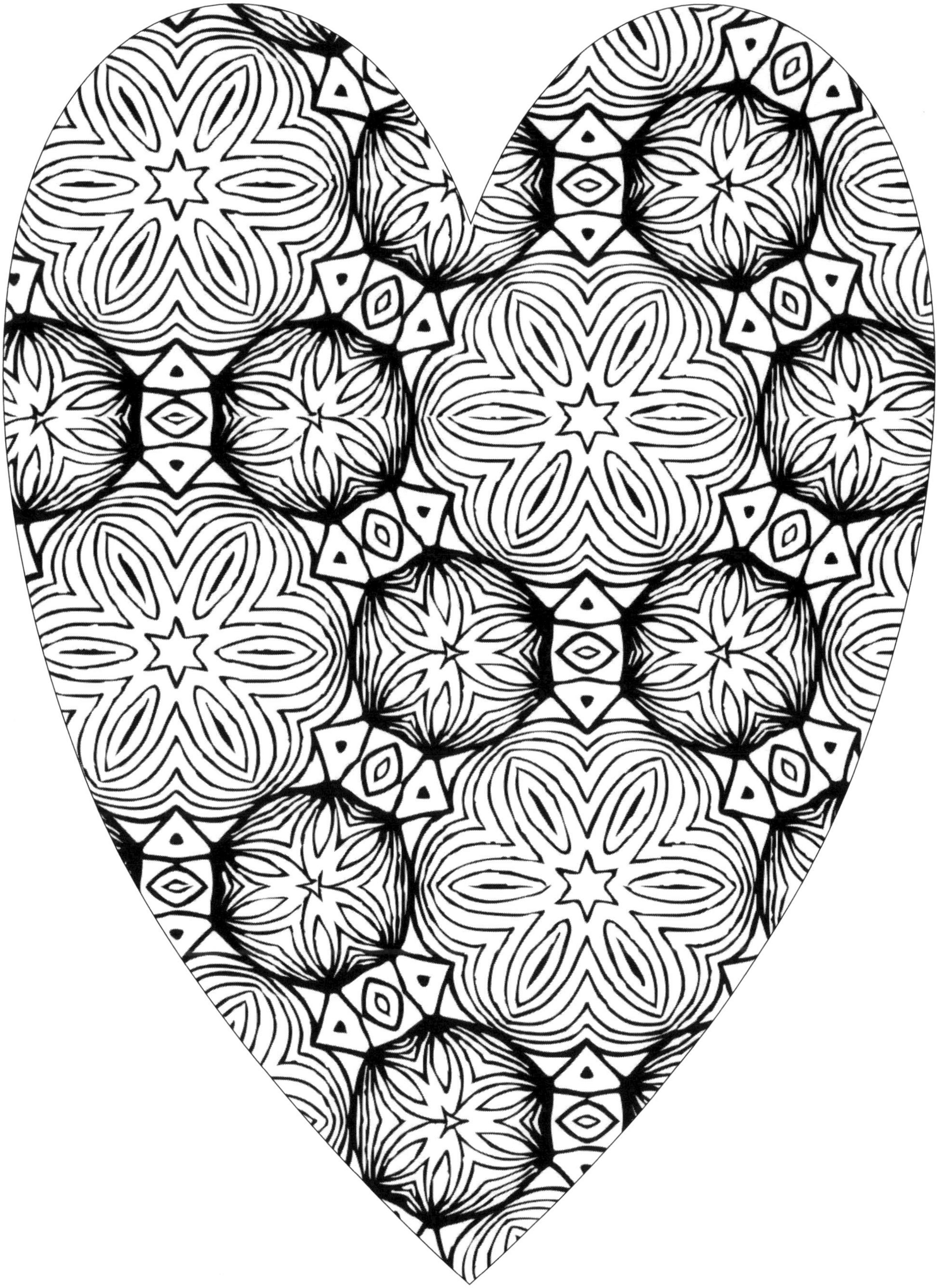

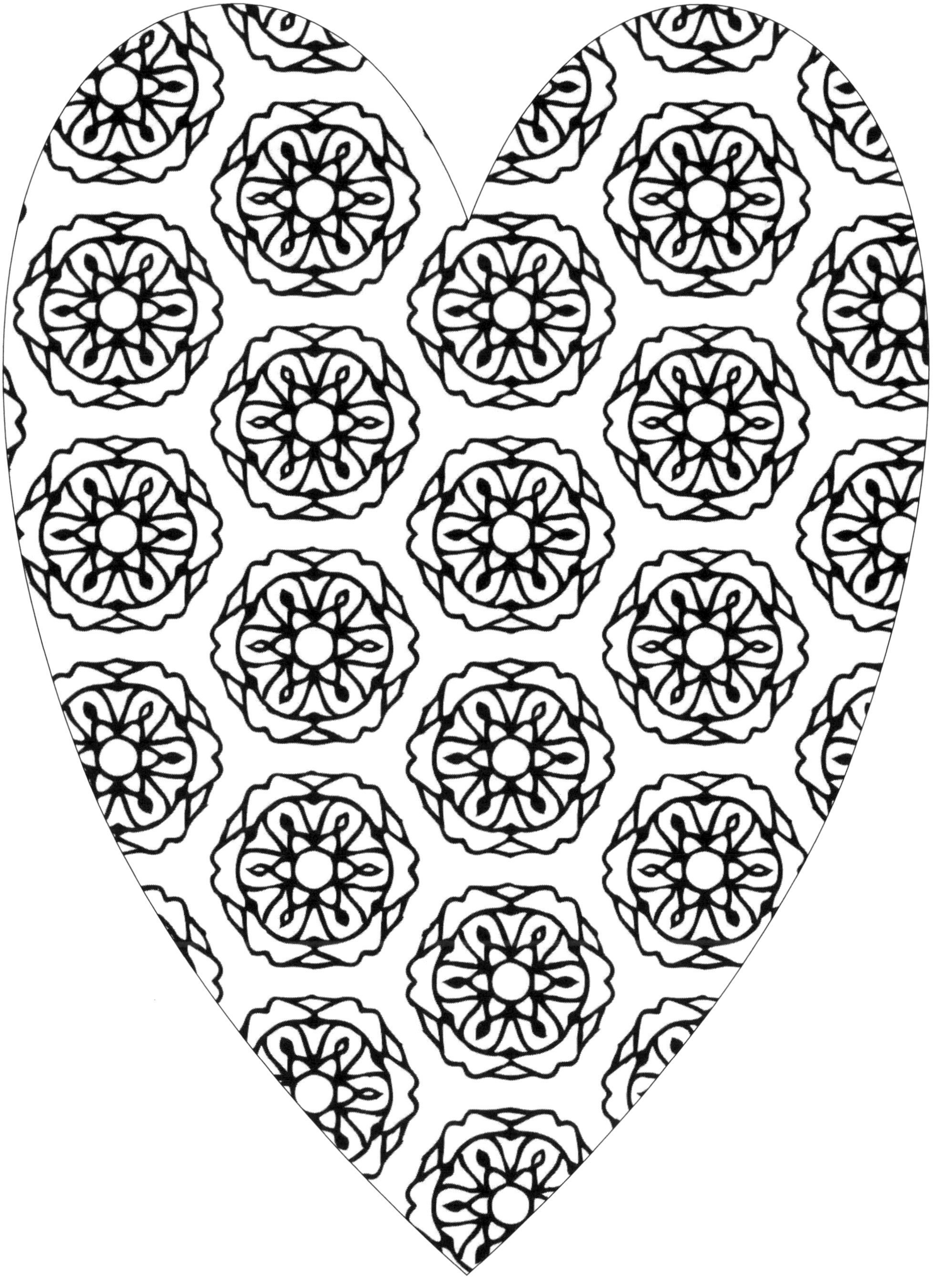

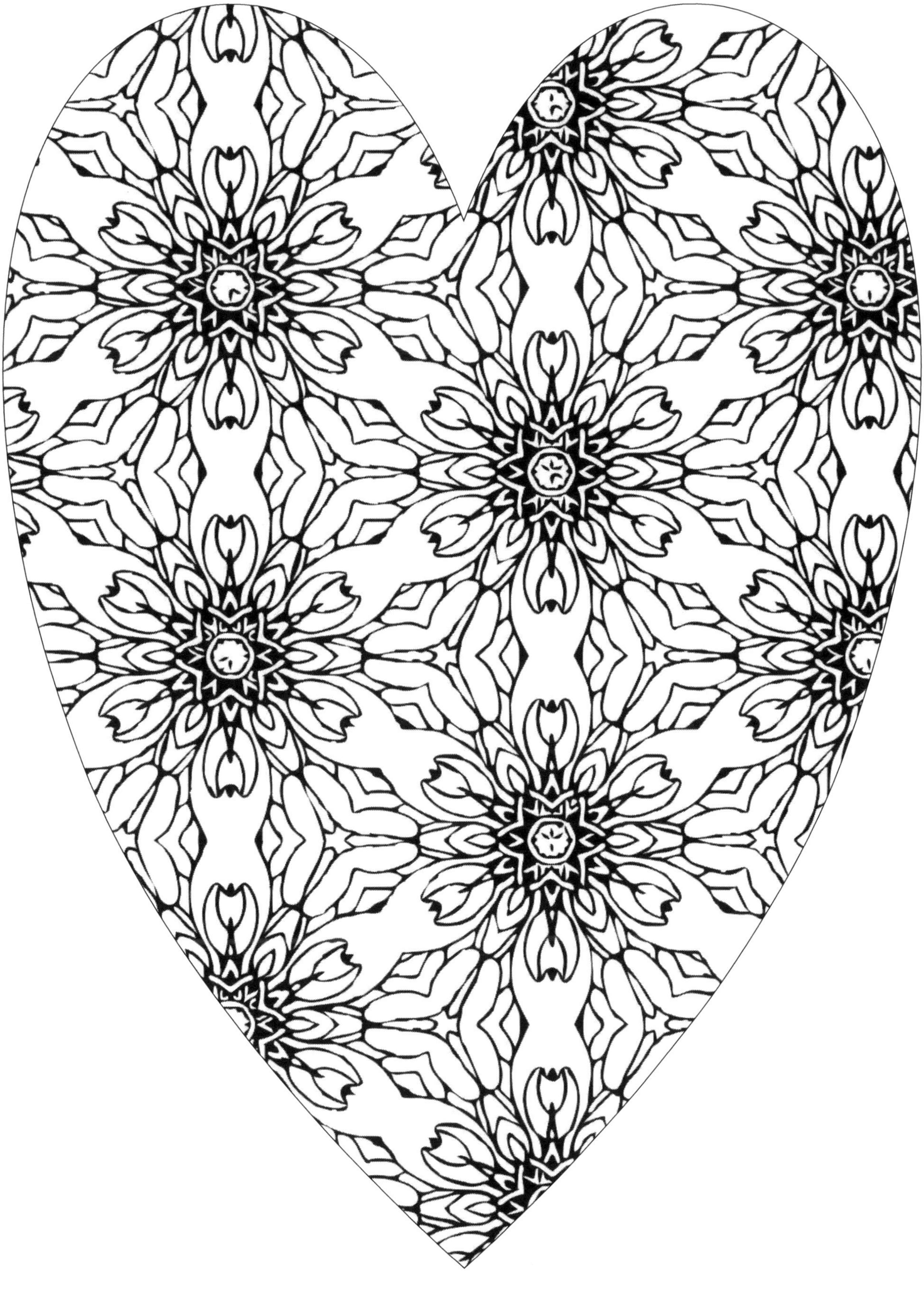

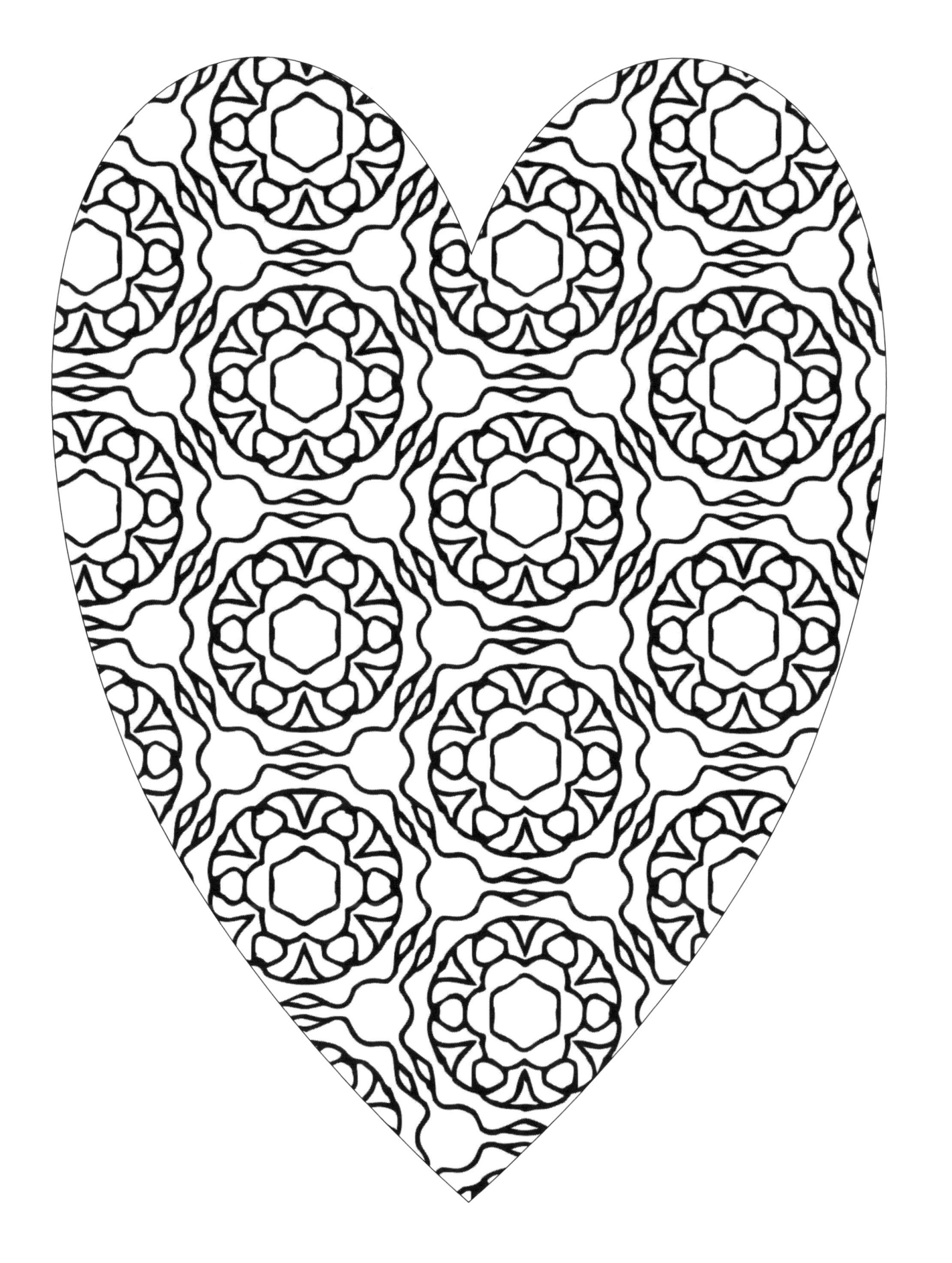

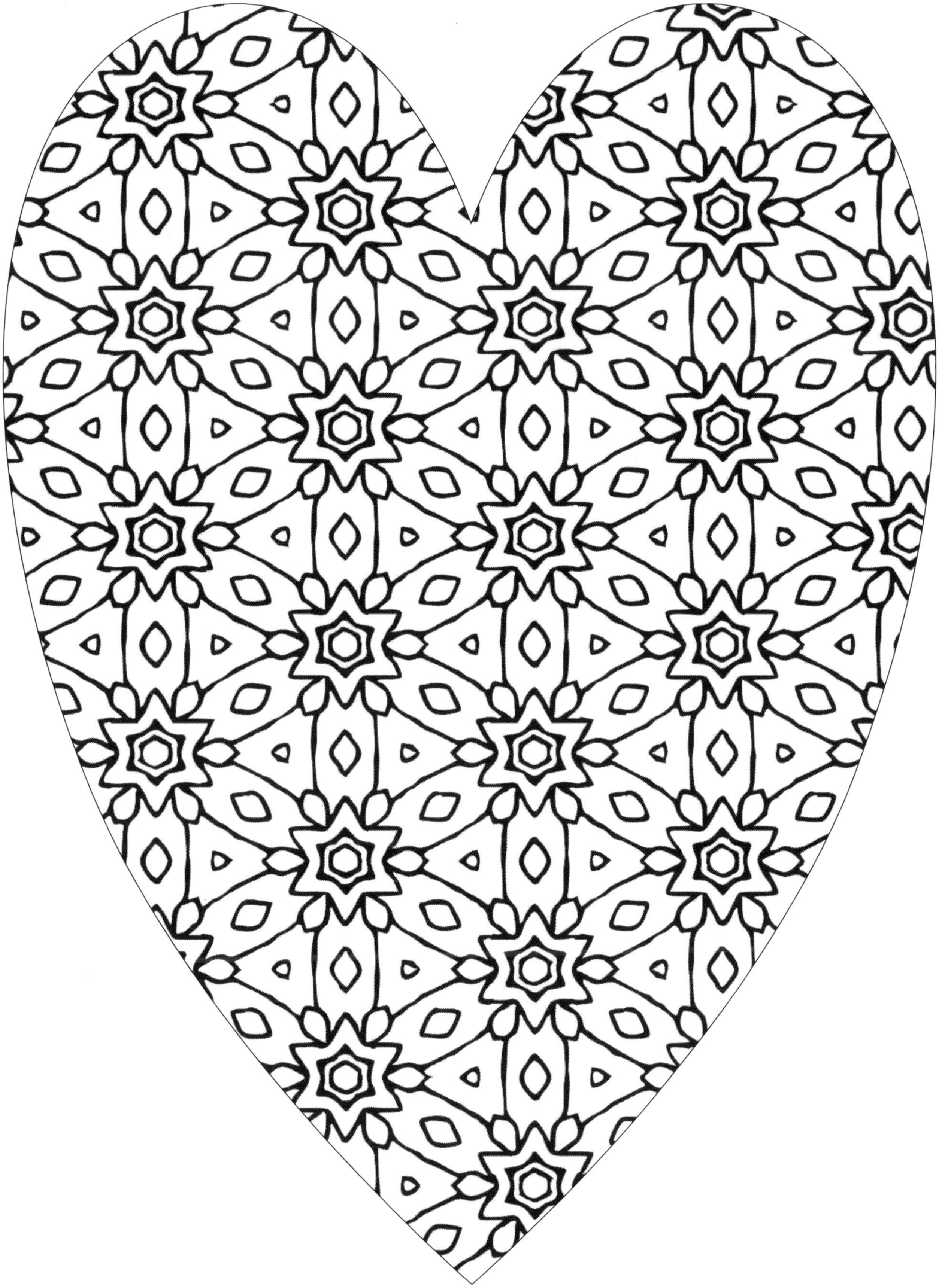

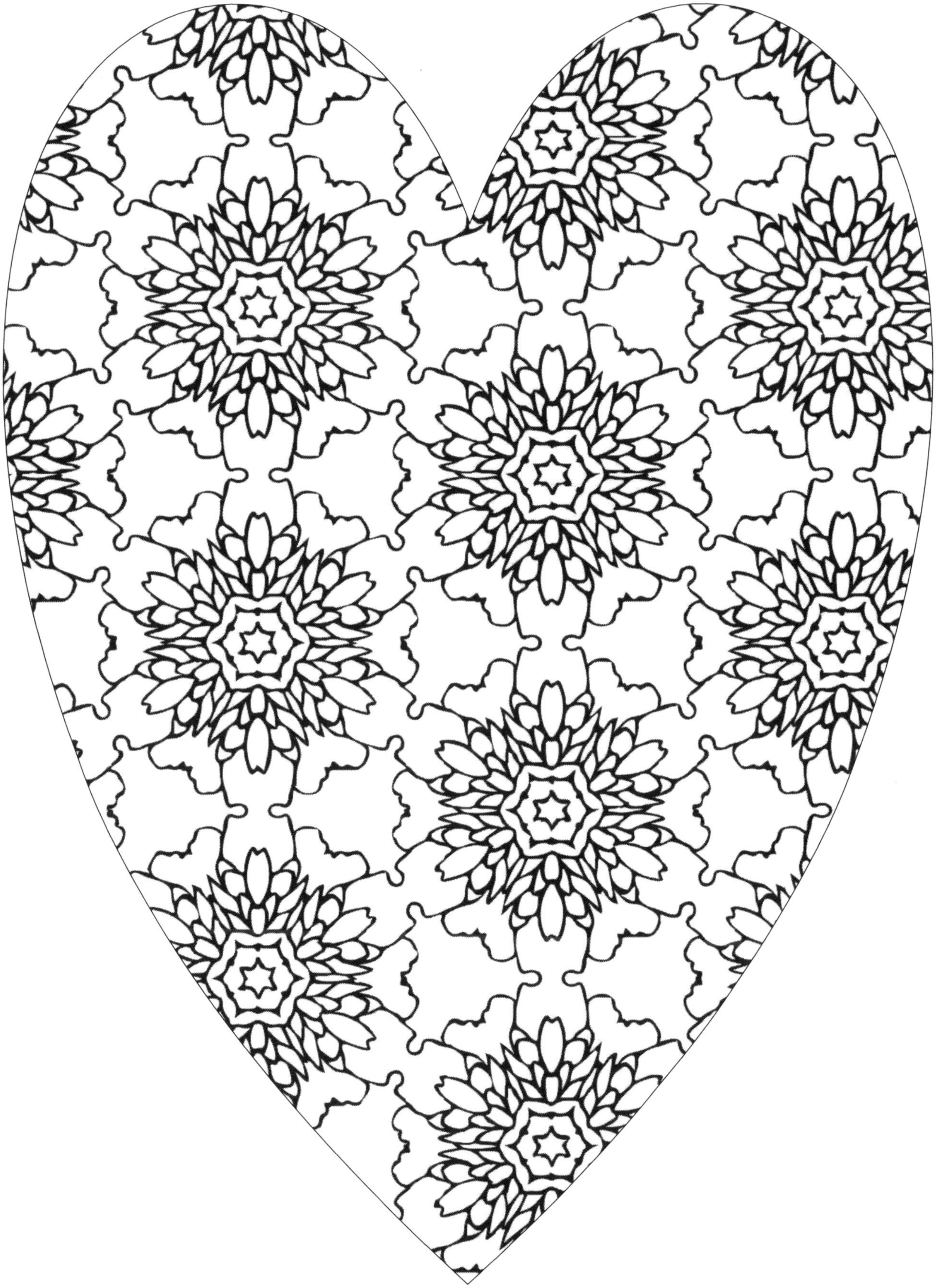

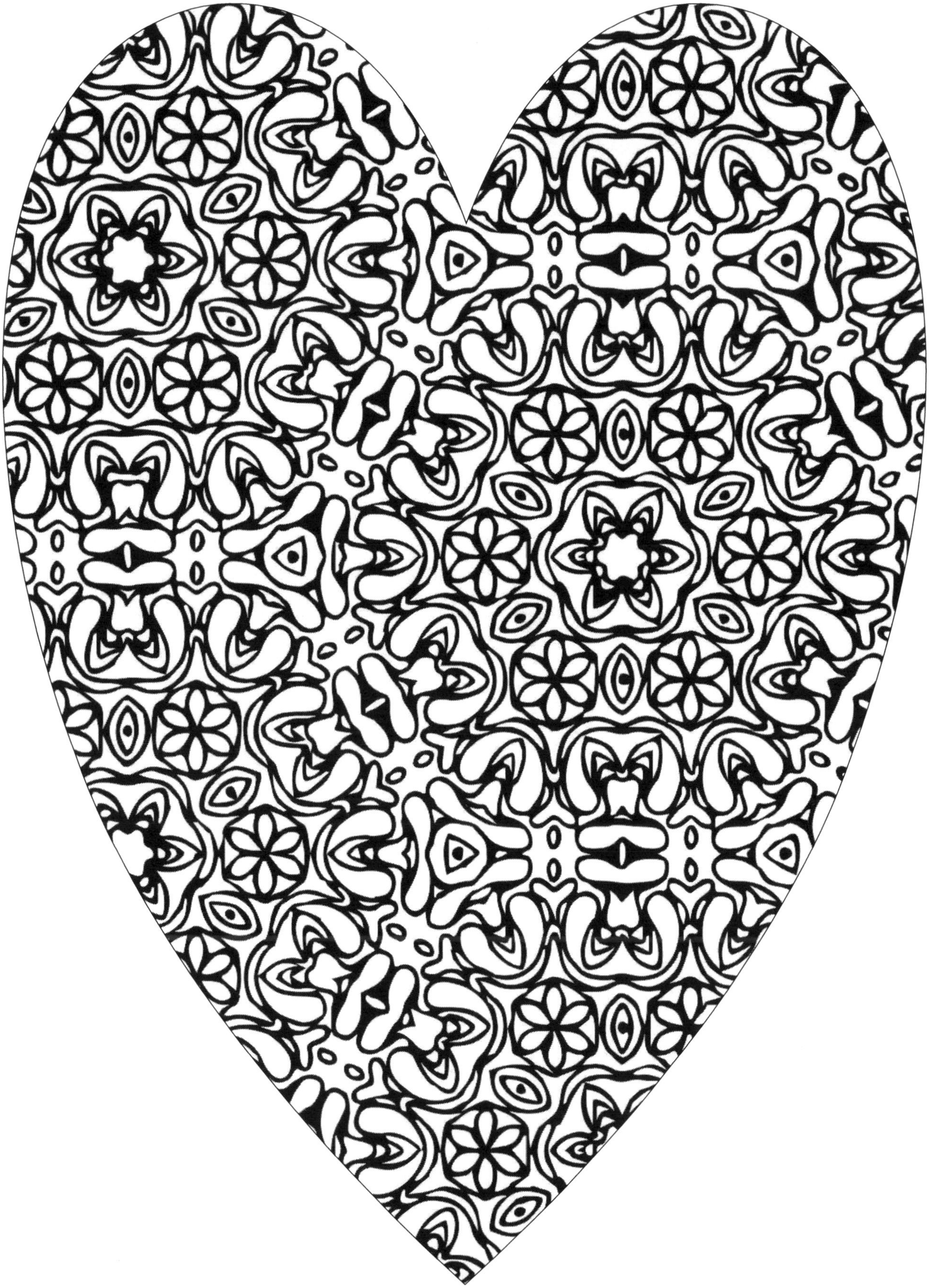

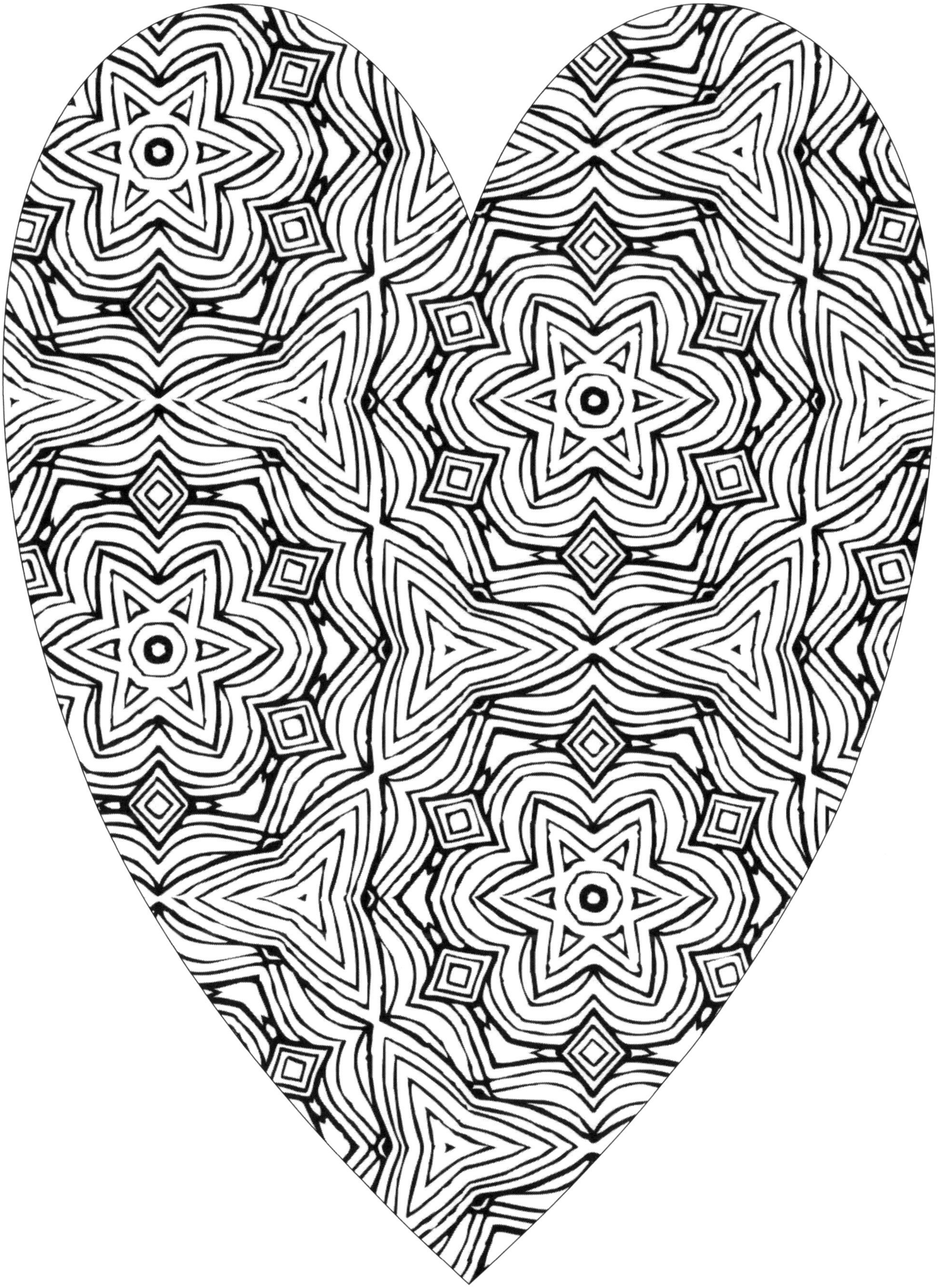

BONUS DETAILS AT END OF PAGE

Thanks for buying my book and your support!

YOU'RE AMAZING

But I still need your help.
If you liked this book would you leave me
a review on Amazon?
(That would be awesome!)
Reviews are so valuable to us Indie Authors.
They help more buyers like you to find us in a
crowded market.
Only 1% of buyers ever leave a review.
If you've got two minutes, please leave a quick review.
I love featuring reviews in my books, blog and emails.
I appreciate you immensely.
Go to your Amazon account and leave a review
for this book there.

BONUS

Get your FREE sampler of colouring patterns

Sign up and subscribe, it's free, to
http://brightboldpublishing.com/mia/

Printed in Great Britain
by Amazon